THE SMART WOMAN'S GUIDE TO PROPERTY LAW

THE SMART WOMAN'S GUIDE TO PROPERTY LAW

Protect Your Assets When You Live with Someone, Marry, Divorce, and More

Carla Spivack

ROWMAN & LITTLEFIELD
Lanham • Boulder • New York • London

Published by Rowman & Littlefield
An imprint of The Rowman & Littlefield Publishing Group, Inc.
4501 Forbes Boulevard, Suite 200, Lanham, Maryland 20706
www.rowman.com

6 Tinworth Street, London SE11 5AL

British Library Cataloguing in Publication Information Available

Library of Congress Cataloging-in-Publication Data

Name: Spivack, Carla, 1961–, author.
Title: The smart woman's guide to property law : protect your assets
    when you live with someone, marry, divorce, and more / Carla Spi-
    vack.
Description: Lanham : Rowman & Littlefield Publishing Group, 2020. |
    Includes bibliographical references and index. | Summary: "The
    Smart Woman's Guide to Property Law shows how current property
    laws cheat women at various stages of life: marriage, caretaking, chil-
    drearing, outliving your spouse, inheritance, and more. Carla Spivack
    illuminates these pitfalls and shows women how to avoid them, pro-
    tect their wealth, and build for the future"—Provided by publisher.
Identifiers: LCCN 2019051341 (print) | LCCN 2019051342 (ebook) |
    ISBN 9781538134917 (cloth) | ISBN 9781538134924 (epub)
Subjects: LCSH: Marital property—United States. | Women—United
    States—Handbooks, manuals, etc.
Classification: LCC KF524 .S65 2020 (print) | LCC KF524 (ebook) |
    DDC 346.7304—dc23
LC record available at https://lccn.loc.gov/2019051341
LC ebook record available at https://lccn.loc.gov/2019051342

∞ ™ The paper used in this publication meets the minimum requirements of American National Standard for Information Sciences Perma-
nence of Paper for Printed Library Materials, ANSI/NISO Z39.48-1992.

For Rachel Spivack, JD,
University of Pennsylvania Law School, 2021

CONTENTS

ACKNOWLEDGMENTS

It's true what authors say. There are so many people whose support, feedback, and patience were essential to this book seeing the light of day. My amazing agent, Barbara Braun, believed in this project and stuck with it through thick and thin. My wonderful editor, Genoveva Llosa, taught me to write in English instead of legalese—and any failures in that regard are mine, not hers! I'm also grateful beyond words for the ongoing support of my colleagues at Oklahoma City University School of Law, in particular Dean Valerie K. Couch, who granted me the initial financial support to start writing, Paula J. Dalley, Michael T. Gibson, and Shannon Roessler, cheerleaders throughout. My assistant, Vickey Cannady, performed miracles of formatting and editing without batting an eye (as usual), and my research assistant, Emma C. Kincaide, diligently and enthusiastically accomplished the tedious task of compiling the index. Ophthalmologists B. Thomas Hutchinson, Claudia U. Richter, and Steven R. Sarkisian have kept my eyes working lo these many years, which really helped.

So many friends and colleagues gave me much needed encouragement and feedback throughout this process: R. B. Bernstein, Amy Boesky, Jessica L. Brown, Naomi R. Cahn, Allison R. Carmody, Elizabeth R. Carter, Loy Corder, Mary Thomas Crane, Susan Carns Curtis, Harold Forsythe, Lawrence Friedman, Deborah

Gordon, Victoria J. Hanneman, Eric B. Hermanson, Debra Jackson, Ray D. Madoff, Seth Markley, Elizabeth Meier, Mimi and Gerry Raphel, Kent D. Schenkel, Harry M. Schuman, Rise Simon, Allison Anna Tait, and Danaya Wright.

Finally, my thanks to Misha and Luba, for encouraging me and putting up with me, through this and everything else.

INTRODUCTION

Two years after Robert and Amy were married, Robert completed his medical degree, and they relocated so he could complete his residency. Amy had an MBA and worked as a program analyst, but shortly after they moved she was diagnosed with fibromyalgia and chronic fatigue syndrome, leading Amy and Robert to agree that she would leave work and stay home full time. They had two children. After nineteen years of marriage, Amy filed for divorce. The court awarded her alimony of $35,000 per year for five years and $20,000 after that for her lifetime, including child support, as well as the title to their home with responsibility for the mortgage, taxes, and repayment of home equity loans. As for Robert's degree, the court awarded Amy 35 percent of the marital portion of Robert's future earnings, which amounted to annual payments to her of $21,288 for a total of $214,400. So Amy, now forty-six, in poor health and absent from the job market for more than seventeen years, must now forego a shared income of about $200,000 per year and support herself on about $40,000.

Does this seem unfair to you? It should. Amy's story is all too common among women seeking divorce today. That's because women are statistically more likely to sacrifice their own professional development to advance their husbands' careers. When a marriage ends in divorce, women often don't get a return on their investment—and are left with less ability to create wealth on their own. Why? Our legal system—specifically property laws—has much to do with it. In the case of divorces like Amy's, courts are supposed to divide family property fairly, taking into account even a stay-at-home spouse's unpaid contribution. But courts often ignore the largest asset of the financially independent spouse (statistically likely to be the man in a heterosexual relationship): his career and professional degree. Most courts refuse to treat a spouse's increasing earning power as the result of an advanced degree as property to be shared with the other spouse at divorce.

And just as women are likely to have their ability to create wealth or hold on to it be limited by the legal system during a divorce, property laws disadvantage women at key stages of their lives: when cohabiting with a man instead of getting married, signing a prenuptial agreement, surviving an abusive relationship, caring for elderly parents, outliving their husbands, and inheriting property.

How is this possible? I've been teaching the history of women and property law for many years, and I wondered the same thing. The story of women and property law is supposed to be one of progress. The law once discriminated overtly against women—not letting them inherit, for example—but all that has changed; now the law treats men and women the same when it comes to acquiring, managing, and transferring property, not to mention pursuing high-paying professions. That should have solved the problem, right? With legal impediments removed, women's and men's assets should have equalized over the years.

But if we're still at thirty-two cents for every dollar men own in wealth, something went wrong. This book explains what, as well as what you can do about it. In a nutshell, the problem is that, while the law has changed, too many other things about the situation of women haven't—the pressure to marry, the uneven distribution of child and eldercare, the difficulty of advancing in a high-paying career while raising kids, women's greater exposure to domestic violence, and the mere fact that women live longer than men—these things have not changed. So by treating men and women the same, the law actually perpetuates inequality. This book explains how—and how you can protect yourself.

To begin, let's review a bit of history, which I'll illustrate through two examples of women whom the law robbed of their property. These two stories of women who fought back have always inspired me.

DISINHERITANCE PAST

Lady Anne Clifford, Countess of Pembroke, Dorset, and Montgomery, was born on the cusp of the century, in 1590, and died in 1676. Descended from one of the most prominent families of the era, Anne Clifford, the daughter of George, Third Earl of Cumberland (1558–1605), and Margaret Russell (1550–1616), spent most of her life fighting to regain family lands that her father had willed to his brother and his brother's male heirs instead of to her. Why? We'll never know for sure. Maybe he thought she wouldn't be able to manage the land or be able to pay off his debts—or wouldn't have the sense of honor to do so, as he assumed his brother would. The law of England was unclear at this time: some authorities favored male over female heirs, even if the males were not direct descendants. Clearly, so did Earl George. Other authorities, however, declared that direct female descendants should inherit land over lateral males like nephews.

Anne believed that as oldest child, she was the legal heiress of her father's estates: her brother Lord Francis died a few weeks before her birth, and her other brother, Lord Robert, died shortly thereafter. In his will of 1598, however, George left his large estates in Westmorland and Yorkshire to Francis, his brother, providing a sum of money and a pension for Anne and treating her as a daughter rather than as heir.

But Anne was as attached to the family estates as anyone else in the family: she saw herself from an early age as a landed heiress, born into a dense network of social duties and rights reaching back to the days of feudalism. In contradiction to her sense of identity, her father's will treated her merely as a daughter in need of a dowry (essentially, that's what his gift to her was). The inheritance of the estate, and the titles that went with it, on the other hand, would have given Anne her own role in the social order.

There was a catch in George's will: the gift her father left her was conditioned on her not contesting the devise of the land to her uncle, which she promptly did. On November 3, 1606, Margaret Russell, Anne Clifford's mother, initiated a claim on Anne's behalf for the estates and the titles that went with them. For the next ten years, the two women together fought legal battles for the land; when Margaret Russell died in 1616, Anne continued the fight despite intense pressure from both her husbands, many powerful men, and even King James I himself to give it up.

Francis, Earl of Cumberland, died in 1641, leaving the estates in the hands of his son, now the Fifth Earl of Cumberland. If he had been as long-lived as his father, or had had male heirs, Anne would have lost all hope of regaining possession of her inheritance. As it happened, however, he died in 1643 with no male heir, and after thirty-eight years, the estates were finally hers. From then until her death in 1676, she engaged in a massive program of building and rebuilding her castles and lands, establishing alms-houses and hospitals, and managing her holdings. When she died, she left the estate to her elder daughter, Margaret, and to her granddaughter, Isabella.

Three hundred years later, in 1892, Vita Sackville-West, a de-scendant of Anne Clifford, was born at Knole House, part of the property passed down from Anne. Because the Sackville family followed traditional English aristocratic inheritance rules, Vita was not allowed to inherit Knole, despite being the only child in the direct line. Instead, her father left it to his nephew, Charles, who became the fourth baron, and eventually gave it to the British National Trust to avoid paying the estate taxes. As part of this process, Vita was forced to sign away all rights to the estate, which she said "nearly broke my heart, putting my signature to what I regarded as a betrayal of all the tradition of my ancestors and the house I loved."

Why was the land so important to these women? Owning the land and the titles that went with it gave them more than income—although it did that. But it also gave them a freestanding place in society, an identity that was separate from their roles as mothers, sisters, daughters, and wives. As a freestanding member of society, Anne had obligations directly to the king, and he had obligations to her. Vita, as owner of her ancestral lands, embodied the long lineage of her family and its role in English history. Without it, she felt adrift, unmoored. My point is that taking women's property does more than deprive women of money—although it does that, as I show throughout the book—it also deprives them of a place in society, a way to shape the world around them and have a lasting identity in it.

In the past, such disinheritance was the norm. Laws that required land to pass to male heirs often prevented women from inheriting land. But even in families that did not own land, women were deprived of wealth and the independence it brings with it. In England and America, women had no legal existence separate from their husbands. Thus, they could not own property, enter into contracts, earn a salary, or inherit property independently. Any property a wife brought with her into the marriage or inherited during the marriage became her husband's property, which he could sell or dispose of without her agreement, while the wife could not dispose of her property without the husband's concurrence. This also meant that property she brought into the marriage could be seized by the husband's creditors. The wife had no right to manage the marital property. The only limit on the husband's ability to sell or give away her property was that he had to leave enough for the wife to live on when he died, unless she agreed otherwise. The wife could not even make a will without the husband's consent, and he could revoke that consent at any time until she died and the will was submitted for probate. The husband could give all of his personal property away by will to someone other than the wife.

Most men in early America died without wills, in which case the widows received only dower—a third of their husband's real property. The problem with dower was that it gave the widow very limited rights. She had no right to sell the land or leave it to her heirs: when she died, the land descended to her husband's children; if there were no children, it went to the husband's heirs, not to any heirs she might have.

This is the tradition that shaped the law of most of the American states—and still does so today, despite many changes. These states are called "separate property states." A few states, called "community property states" developed from a different tradition, that of France and Spain, which saw marriage as a commercial partnership and which counted any property that came into the marriage as belonging to both spouses equally. This sounds fairer, doesn't it? In some ways it is, but the law of community property states still cheats women of wealth even today—as I'll show.

The property laws affecting women have changed in many important ways. In the 1830s the states began to pass laws called "Women's Property Acts." These laws made property a woman brought into the marriage her separate property, and any property she earned, acquired, or inherited during the marriage would also be hers. Women could now control real property, inherit, participate in lawsuits, and keep their own earnings. Importantly, these laws protected the wife's property from her husband's creditors.

Next, in the 1850s, new laws began to replace dower with gender-neutral schemes, which left equal amounts to whichever spouse survived the other. These replaced earlier laws that often favored men, by either imposing primogeniture or giving a double portion to the eldest son. Now, whoever survived received an equal share. These laws only went so far, however. Most importantly, they gave the wife no property rights in the labor she contributed to the household. For example, when, after thirty years of marriage, Sarah Lewis sought a divorce from her husband on the grounds of "cruel and inhuman treatment" in 1922, she claimed a 365-acre tract of land to which she held title. The court awarded the land to her husband, however, because he had furnished the money to buy it. Sarah argued that the land was "paid for out of both our work" and that her labor in raising eleven children and tending to her husband's store "ought to be worth something," but the court disagreed, stating, "It plainly appears that the wife had no interest whatever in the land except as the spouse of her husband. She neither bought nor paid for it."

The court reasoned that Sarah's labor gave her no claim on the land because the wife's performance of household labor was a duty imposed on her by the common law, and any contract to pay her for it would not only be void but also be against public policy. Sarah Lewis was not the only wife who sought compensation for household labor: after the Married Women's Property Acts were passed, many women began to claim rights in property gained partly because of their work in the home. Courts across the board rejected these claims. As I will show, the law has not resolved this problem adequately today. Women still perform more household labor today, labor that often enables their husbands to acquire assets, and family property law still fails to fully compensate them for it. Although some courts have taken tentative steps to give wives some compensation for their unpaid labor, the doctrine of household labor as uncompensated duty surreptitiously remains. It appears when women are denied compensation for labor that enables their partners to be "model workers" who can be available for work at all hours of the day, travel regularly for work, or start a business—because the couple was not formally married, or because the wife had signed away her rights to marital assets before her years of contribution, or because the law deems caring for family members uncompensated because it is a duty.

To summarize: While in the past our laws were used to openly discriminate against women—for example, by preventing women from owning their own property outright—over the past century and a half the laws have changed to treat women equally to men. Sounds great, right? Except, as we've already seen, these changes have not resulted in women's equal property ownership. This is because, while treating men and women equally on its face, the law still plays out in real life in a discriminatory fashion because men and women are often not equal when it comes to income, career opportunities, and caregiving. Women are more likely to take time off from work to give birth and take care of children. Even if they continue working part time or full time, they are more likely to take on more household duties, the bulk of child-rearing, and caregiving responsibilities for their elderly parents than are men. All of these sacrifices severely affect their *income*—in the form of lower salaries—and their *wealth* (their total financial assets minus debt)—in the form of their ability to invest in their career and start or grow a business, increase their earning potential, and fatten their retirement and investments accounts.

In short, women are more likely statistically to be in a financially dependent relationship with their male partners. Meanwhile, men are not only free from the same social limiting factors that keep women behind but also often *benefit* from women's sacrifices that enable men to invest more heavily in their careers by being available for work at all hours of the day, including traveling or starting a business. Their incomes grow, and more importantly their wealth grows.

The income gap between women and men has gotten lots of attention in the last few decades: today women earn seventy-nine cents for every dollar men earn. But fewer people are aware of the much more serious wealth gap: for every dollar in wealth men own, women own thirty-two cents. Yes, let's rewind: thirty-two cents for every dollar men own.

Wealth matters. Wealth is what gives us a financial safety net when we lose our jobs, break up a relationship or divorce, our dependents or we become sick, or we are hit by some other financial crisis. It enables us to build security, to give our children a future, and to retire. It is passed from generation to generation, allowing wealthy families to *stay* wealthy over time. Wealth can generate income, whether through investments in the financial markets, real estate, funding a startup business, and more. Significant wealth even allows us to influence our world by contributing to political campaigns and policy initiatives. For these reasons, wealth is a better indicator of financial status than income: it reveals who is secure and influential and who is not, who can weather the storms of life, and who can have an effect on the world around them and who can't.

By treating women and men equally without recognizing the gross social and economic advantages that differentiate us, the law perpetuates the wealth gap. I would go as far as arguing that it cheats women out of their wealth.

The Smart Woman's Guide to Property Law lays the blame for the wealth gap where it belongs—on the legal system—and helps women avoid the pitfalls in the law that deprive them of their rightful share of wealth. The book explains how the laws disadvantage women who are going through six difficult life events where the distribution of wealth and property comes into play:

- Breaking up with someone they've cohabited with. The law does not protect you! A court will divide property and order spousal support when necessary if a couple was married, but without a formal marriage, the law will often not intervene.
- Negotiating prenuptial agreements. The court will very likely enforce these even if you feel you signed it under duress—for example, if it was the day before the wedding or if you were pregnant and had no home, job, or insurance.
- Going through divorce. If you gave up your career or advanced education to support your husband's professional or business development, the law will probably not adequately compensate you for it.
- Surviving domestic and, especially, financial abuse. Financial exploitation is part of spousal abuse, and you need to understand ways the law will and will not help you protect your wealth.
- Caring for an elderly or sick family member. This is mostly done by women, and the law isn't very helpful in getting women compensation for it to make up for cutting back on careers.
- Outliving their spouse and inheriting part of their estate. There are many gaps in the law when it comes to making

sure the surviving spouse—likely the wife—gets a fair share of the estate that reflects the partnership of the marriage.

Although I do offer practical advice on how women can protect themselves and their wealth from unfair laws in the life events listed above, this is not a how-to book on divorce, prenup agreements, estate planning, and so on. And while much of the information and advice in the book will apply to some degree to whoever is the financially vulnerable party in a legal dispute over property—which could be a man or a woman in an opposite-sex or a same-sex relationship—I write primarily to women in relationships with men since, statistically speaking, they are more likely to find themselves disadvantaged by the law.

This book is also not meant to teach you the law. You can easily look up your state's laws on the internet. But you have to know what the legal issues are so you can know what to research—that's what this book is for. I flag the areas of law that could rob you of wealth and explain how they work and what to look out for. I hope to empower you by warning you about the pitfalls in law.

Certainly we have come a long way when it comes to how the law treats us and our wealth. When my mother, Charlotte Spivack, was hired along with my father by the University of Massachusetts at Amherst as a professor of English in 1964, the university's policy was to pay women in the same department as their husbands half-time pay, even though they worked full time. This situation persisted until the passage of Title VII—the federal law that prohibits employers from discriminating against employees on the basis of sex, race, color, national origin, and religion—when a letter from my mother's attorney got her a raise and a check for back pay by return mail.

It's also crucial to understand that issues of family and property are almost all matters of state law. Each state has its own laws regarding cohabitation, property division on divorce, prenups, inheritance, and compensation for caregiving. The law from state to state can—and does—vary greatly. Some states will come off much worse than others in this book (Mississippi). Here are some illustrations of just how diverse these results can be: given a nine-teen-year marriage, no children, with the husband earning $125,000 and the wife earning $25,000, alimony awards ranged from $23,500 to $41,667—so a 50 percent difference—and the duration of the awards varied from three years to a lifetime—all depending on the state.

The stories I tell in this book are worst-case scenarios; in many of them the outcome might have been different in a different state—or even a different county, court, or before a different judge. These matters are very local, and judges in family courts have a large amount of discretion—meaning they are quite free to use their own sense of what is fair in a given situation. This can lead to widely varying results, as you can imagine. So nothing in this book should be taken to say that the law has not made progress—and in some states a lot of progress—and that it's not possible for women to get fair treatment in court in the situations I describe.

But.

We still have a longer way to go. In my ten years' 'teaching about women and property law at Oklahoma City University School of Law, I've met countless women who have had their wealth siphoned away as property laws failed to protect their inter-ests or acknowledge their situations. Their stories, and my re-search and writing on women and the law, have led me to advo-cate for legal change: the law must recognize inequalities and differences between men and women, not pretend they don't ex-ist. It must stop enforcing prenuptial agreements that are grossly unfair, it must be willing to divide property among couples that have lived together and raised children without marriage, it should treat professional degrees as property that can be shared upon divorce, and it must close the loopholes that allow a spouse to disinherit his surviving partner. Ignoring inequality won't get rid of it. The law must play an active role in eradicating it.

And—

Why take chances? Maybe you live in a progressive state with laws that treat the financially dependent person fairly (or maybe you live in Mississippi). Either way, why let someone else decide your fate? Women also have to take an active role in protecting their wealth from the pitfalls of the law. I hope this book will arm them with the information they need to make that happen for themselves.

A NOTE ABOUT NOTES

The stories I tell in this book are ones I took from actual legal cases. I did not change or embellish the facts in any way. Each case reference is given in the note. You can usually find these cases by simply Googling the reference I give in the note.

FINALLY . . .

On a final note, I admit up front that this book is based on the model of an opposite-sex marriage; it is in this scenario that the woman is likely—though not necessarily—the financially dependent spouse. It's often the case that one partner in a same-sex marriage might be less financially independent than the other, and this book will be useful for that person as well—it is useful for anyone in that situation. Since the book is about women, and gender, I have kept to the heterosexual model throughout, but this is not meant to deny the existence of other couples—or the wonderful variety of families in America today.

1

THE LEGAL PITFALLS
OF LIVING TOGETHER

Catherine and Eugene lived together for twenty-four years and had a child together.[1] After their daughter was born in 1992, they agreed that Catherine would stay home and raise her, as well as care for the house, do the shopping, cooking, and all other housekeeping chores, while Eugene pursued "various entrepreneurial efforts," including setting up his own corporation. According to Catherine, Eugene had a domineering personality and much superior bargaining power and in this way managed to get sole title to all their assets, even ones they had acquired through joint efforts. In 2004, after twenty-four years, Eugene suddenly decided to end the relationship and told Catherine to leave their home.

Catherine wanted compensation for all the years she had worked in the home without pay, enabling Eugene to build his company and become wealthy. She demanded that the court divide the property they had acquired through a combination of their joint efforts and back pay for all of her uncompensated labor. But the trial court wouldn't hear her claims—why? Because they weren't formally married. Catherine appealed. The appellate court wouldn't hear her either—same reason. It said there was no law granting rights of property division to unmarried partners, and there was nothing it could do about it unless the legislature decided to change that. So, after twenty-four years of building what she thought was a life together, Catherine was left with nothing to show for it.

Like Catherine, you might be one of the many women who are choosing to live with their partners rather than marry—or as a prelude to getting married. Living together or "cohabiting" might be a good test of how well you get along at close quarters or a gentle way to start blending your separate lives. Or it might be an alternative to a legal institution you don't believe in or feel you can support.

Whatever your reason for moving in together, it is a big milestone in your emotional relationship with your partner: it deepens your commitment to each other, to the relationship itself, and to building a life together. During this exciting time, it might seem terribly unromantic to think about the legal ramifications of commingling your lives, finances, and even property. But it's crucial that you do.

Since 1995, more and more couples are choosing to live together or cohabit—and they are increasingly having children together outside of marriage (although many of these children are unplanned).[2] Of these couples, only about 40 percent of them will ever marry.[3] As in legal marriages, women in these informal relationships are more likely than men to sacrifice getting an education and advancing their careers and to take on childcare and housekeeping responsibilities so their male partners can focus on increasing their earning potential and wealth. They assume that wealth will benefit and be enjoyed by both.

But there's a big difference between married people and those who cohabit. The law extends married people certain rights, such as court-supervised property division and spousal maintenance upon divorce, inheritance rights, social security survivor's benefits in the event their spouses die, or the right to sue a third party for damages in a wrongful death case. But it won't necessarily do so for people who just lived with their partners. Some states do extend certain rights to cohabitants, but others do not. And no matter what, in every case, the court has a lot of discretion.

The law does much more (although still often not enough) to protect the financially dependent partner (usually the woman) should the marriage end. When you cohabit, if you split up or your partner dies, the courts will often not step in to divide the property or the wealth you helped create fairly as it would if you had been married. If you've made professional or financial sacrifices such as working without pay to help your partner start a business or postponing your career to stay home with kids—on the assumption that you were building a permanent life together—you may be left with little to show for those sacrifices.

While some courts *will* divide property between two people who have lived together, they often require a legally valid contract between them before they will do so. The problem, though, is that very few couples have written contracts—even fewer have *legally valid* ones, written in specific, technical legal language you probably don't know about. (A court might not consider a contract valid even though you and your partner thought it was!)

If you are living or planning to live with someone, do you have a legally valid contract with that person? Are you willing to ask for one?

If you answered no to the first question—and you have already made financial sacrifices for the relationship, or plan to—you are at significant risk if the relationship breaks up. Statistically speaking, unfortunately, the relationship likely will end if it doesn't result in marriage in five years or less.[4] If you answered yes to the second question—and I hope you did— read on.

In this chapter, I explore how property laws are particularly unfair to women who cohabit and cheat them of wealth that is rightfully theirs. I also explain how cohabitation is often informally but *incorrectly* referred to or assumed to be the same as "common law marriage," which offers some protections but is available in only nine states (and D.C.). Finally, I show how women can protect themselves from being cheated in cohabitation situations with some tips on how to prepare binding contracts with their partners.

THE MYTH OF COMMON LAW MARRIAGE (AND DOMESTIC PARTNERSHIPS)

If you've lived with your partner for seven or more years, you might be thinking, *Wait a second, aren't I technically in "a common law marriage?"* The answer is simple: no. A few states recognize common law marriage, but the length of time you've lived together has no direct bearing on it.

Before I go into this more, let's distinguish between common law marriage and living together. If you agree to live with your partner without getting married, you are cohabiting. Lots of people simply live together. "Cohabitation" is the legal term for this living arrangement.

Common law marriage, on the other hand, is what we call a "legal doctrine." It refers to two people who share their lives and assets—maybe raise children together—and here's the crucial part: *they actually think of themselves as married.* They tell people around them that they are married; they refer to each other and introduce each other as "husband" or "wife"; they file joint tax returns and have joint bank accounts; one of them may take the other partner's last name; and generally they hold themselves out to the community as a couple who has been formally married. Your friends and neighbors must think they are, in fact, married.

Currently, only nine states (and the District of Columbia) recognize common law marriages by statute or case law,[5] and proving that you are in one can be very hard. It's not enough to simply move in with your partner. And there isn't a magical number of years a couple must live together (seven is often inaccurately thrown around) after which the couple automatically enters into a common law marriage.[6] Your relationship must fulfill specific requirements to be considered a common law marriage—and these requirements differ from state to state.

You might also have heard of domestic partnerships. These are also different from common law marriages and from plain cohabiting. Domestic partners are two people who live together, without marrying, and who might be entitled to some of the same rights and benefits as married couples. As with common law marriages, it's not as simple as declaring yourself part of a domestic partnership. Domestic partners have to *register* with the state they live in. And as with common law marriages, not all states recognize domestic partnerships. Until the Supreme Court legalized same-sex marriage, in some states, domestic partners' rights were reserved for same-sex couples. States that have domestic partnership laws for *opposite*-sex couples today are California, Hawaii, Maine, Maryland, Nevada, New Hampshire, New Jersey, Oregon, Washington, and Wisconsin.

Domestic partnerships are limited in various ways. For example, California's registry, which grants registered couples the same rights and responsibilities as married couples in the state, is limited to couples in which at least one partner is over sixty-two. The most comprehensive registry is that of the District of Columbia, which applies to all registered couples without any age requirements and gives registered couples identical rights to spouses with regard to inheritance, spousal immunity, spousal support, property division upon termination of the relationship, and the right to sue for wrongful death. Other states offer much more limited rights.

Of course, if you and your partner have decided to live together instead of marrying, you are also unlikely to want to register as a legal obligated partnership. Now that same-sex marriage is legal in every state, these registries really only serve a purpose for the small number of people who decline to marry for ideological reasons, such as political objections to the institution of marriage itself. If you are opting to live together for this reason, by all means, register if your state allows it. It will give you more rights than you would have without it.

The key takeaway is that the law treats cohabitation, common law marriages, and domestic partnerships very differently when these relationships dissolve. For the purpose of property division and inheritance, domestic partnerships and common law marriages might be treated the same as a regular marriage by those states that recognize them. But chances are you are either not registered with your state as a domestic partner or don't live in a state that recognizes common law marriage—or you do but don't meet your state's requirements for one.

You are most likely plain "cohabiting." And the law does not treat the financially vulnerable cohabitant very kindly when it comes to the distribution of property. Some states have laws that allow for it, while other states' laws make it much harder. It all comes down to which state you live in and whether you had a contract with the person you are splitting from—and what *kind* of contract you have.

IT'S ALL ABOUT THE CONTRACT

If you are living with someone, you should find out how the law treats cohabitation in your state. Do so even if you are happy in your relationship and don't foresee it ever ending. Relationships change. People change. The minute you start cohabiting with someone, your lives—including your finances—begin to commingle. It's always good to understand how the law where you live would handle the division of property and assets that you've accumulated with that person. It pays to be prepared.

Some states make it harder than others to divide property between cohabiting partners. For example, the Illinois Supreme Court recently affirmed that courts in that state will not divide property between unmarried cohabitants. Other states will divide property even if you don't have any kind of cohabiting contract; in the absence of a contract, they'll divide property based simply on fairness to each party. Courts in Arizona, California, Connecticut, Florida, Hawaii, Indiana, Iowa, Kansas, Missouri, Nevada, New Jersey, North Carolina, Pennsylvania, Vermont, Washington, West Virginia, and Wisconsin seem willing to recognize property rights between unmarried cohabitants and will sometimes divide property based on notions of fairness, even without explicit contracts. In these states, therefore, you don't need anything in writing, or even an explicit agreement, to get some kind of property division, if fairness seems to require it.[7] But you're still better off with a written contract: your idea of fair property division might not be the same as the court's—and not as fair as what you could have worked out with your own contract.

Alaska, Maryland, Nebraska, Oregon, and Wyoming will enforce express or implied agreements between unmarried couples. These agreements can be in writing or not, and they can be clearly stated between the parties or simply "understood." For example, you might both understand that it made more sense for you to stay home with the kids while he advanced in his career, without ever making an express contract about how you might be compensated if you broke up. The problem with this situation, of course, is that unless there is a written contract, it comes down to he-said, she-said, and it's up to the court to decide whom to believe.[8]

Kentucky, Michigan, Minnesota, Mississippi, New Hampshire, New Mexico, New York, North Dakota, and Ohio will only enforce express agreements—in writing or expressly agreed to by the parties.[9]

It doesn't really matter what state you are in. You need a written contract for support and property division in case of separation.

Let's look at each kind of contract more closely.

Written Contracts

Hands down, the best thing you can do to protect yourself and your wealth when you are living with another person is to have a written agreement or what's called a "cohabitation agreement." This written contract—which needs to be signed by you and your partner—spells out what each of you owns separately, what property and assets you share or will share (especially those acquired during the relationship), how these will be divided, how you will support each other financially if you break up, and more. In fact, some states like Minnesota, New Jersey, North Dakota, and Texas require that if you have a contract with your partner, it must be in writing to be enforceable.

If you are like most women who live with a partner, you probably don't have a written cohabitation contract. Most women rarely think to ask for one—or don't think they need one because they
believe they'll never break up with their significant other. If this is
you, I truly hope you're right about the breaking up part. More
important, however, I find that the more committed people are to
each other, the more likely they are to have written agreements
about sharing property and support. Does that seem counterintui-
tive? I don't think it is. Think about it: if both people are truly
committed to building a life together through combined effort and
sacrifice, it would make sense that they would be happy to memo-
rialize it in writing as an expression of that mutual commitment,
and as a way to make sure the details were ironed out so it would
work smoothly. On the other hand, you can see that if one partner
were less committed than the other, he or she might balk at the
idea of a something in writing.

If you have a contract—great! You are one step ahead. But it's
critical that you verify that your contract is *legally* valid. Courts can
be picky about enforcing contracts that do not comply with legal
technicalities, especially when you face a judge who doesn't like
people living together outside of marriage (you would be surprised
how much a judge's bias—whatever it is—matters in these cases).
For example, if the contract looks anything like a bargain for sex, it
will be invalid because that's illegal.

See what I mean? Details matter when drafting an enforceable
contract. At the end of this chapter, I offer some guidance on how
to write an agreement that will stand up in court.

Express Oral Contracts

In the course of your relationship, it's likely you've had many
conversations with you partner about what you expect of each
other, including about financial matters now and in the future. In
the absence of a written contract, some states will recognize and
enforce such a spoken agreement between you and your partner.

But many states will only do so if the oral contract is "express"—that is, if you explicitly agreed on the financial terms of your relationship.

Expressly agreeing to the terms of the relationship means that at some point you and your partner sat down and talked about specifically, and verbally agreed on, who will do what: who will work outside the home, do most of housekeeping, take care of children, pay for your home rent or mortgage, and pay the utility bills—and how you would divide your assets if you split up—who would keep what, how you would divide your property, retirement accounts, and so on.

Oral contracts are by far the most common form of agreement that couples living together have. The trouble is that it's much easier for one person to deny their existence: since it's not in writing, there is often no proof. And even if both partners agree that there was some kind of contract, they can argue about what the terms were. It's your word against your former partner's. This is not a good situation to be in.

Implied Contracts

Perhaps you and your partner never sat down and agreed explicitly about how you would share your finances and property while living together. But nonetheless you've assumed that you *were* in agreement. For example, you might have assumed that the house you lived in together and for which you contributed half the down payment and mortgage payments would be divided equally if you broke up—even if the house was in your partner's name only. In legal terms, this is called an implied contract: neither of you made an express promise, but the fact that you had an unspoken agreement is clear from the way you both acted, and you counted on that unspoken but obvious agreement.

Like express oral contracts, implied ones are difficult to prove. But just as problematic is the fact that what you think your implied contract with your partner is might not be what a court thinks it is.

Take the case of Sabrina and Bruce, who began living together in August 1988 when Sabrina had just turned seventeen and was still in high school and Bruce was twenty-eight and earning $9.00 per hour working at an electric company. At the time, the parties lived in a small rental home and their combined net worth was less than $2,000. [10]

A year after they moved in together, Bruce earned his electrician's license. Sabrina dropped out of high school because Bruce suggested she accompany him to job sites so they could both learn the electric business and start a business of their own in the future. Bruce and Sabrina worked together every day, sometimes for up to twelve hours.

Over the next four years, Bruce and Sabrina built up their electrical business together. Bruce performed the licensed electrical work, and Sabrina wired boxes and stuffed plugs. She also trained electrical helpers, handled the company's billing and payroll, and supervised job sites when Bruce was not available to do so. Sabrina never requested any kind of hourly compensation for her work—meaning she was accumulating no Social Security or retirement pension of her own. Also, during this time, she maintained their home and did all the cooking and cleaning.

In September 1993, Sabrina gave birth to their daughter, Jane. At this point, Sabrina cut back on most of the work she did for the electrical business and devoted her time to taking care of the baby. Shortly after J. was born, the parties opened a joint checking account in the name of Bruce and Sabrina Gazvoda. Bruce deposited the business's income into the account, and Sabrina paid the bills.

Two years later, in 1995, Bruce incorporated the electrical services business as Bruce's Electric Services, Inc. The following year, Bruce started a limited liability company, Bruce's Investment Properties, which included several rental properties that Bruce built. Sabrina had significant responsibilities for the rental properties, including managing and maintaining them.

During the relationship, Bruce and Sabrina discussed marriage on several occasions. Bruce always told Sabrina that the businesses and assets belonged to both of them and that marriage was just a piece of paper—no need for any formalities between them.

This was all well and good until 2004, when Sabrina and Bruce separated. At this point the company they had built together was worth one million. Suddenly, it turned out that marriage certificate was a pretty important piece of paper. Sabrina asked a court for her share of the business and the worth of the work she had put into it—which she estimated at more than $700,000. The trial court awarded her $250,000, about a quarter of what the business was worth at the time of separation and without any compensation for its future earnings. The court refused to award Sabrina half the business she had helped build. It said that all the talk about sharing and everything belonging to both of them was not enough to create a legitimate expectation of a fifty-fifty split; it also said that Bruce had obviously put more work into the business than Sabrina had.

The only way the court could come to this conclusion was to ignore all of Sabrina's housekeeping and childcare work over the years. While you might argue that she was the one without the professional license, and that stuffing electric plugs isn't as much of a contribution as wiring the electricity, all her housekeeping and childcare, in addition to all her work on the job sites, surely made up half of the value of the company—after all, it would have been pretty hard for Bruce to get to work every day without breakfast, clothes, and someone to stay home with the baby. But courts do tend to ignore these contributions. And don't forget—Sabrina dropped out of high school to join forces with Bruce and build a life together. So now, not only is she left with no assets and no home, but also she has no job skills or even a high school degree.

Sabrina's story underscores the problems with implied contracts. First, there's no proof—it's your word against your partner's. Second, even if both of you agree that there was some implied agreement for a trade-off, you and a court might not agree about what those terms are. In Sabrina's case, the court did not agree that there was an implied agreement of equal sharing of what they had built together if they broke up.

The kind of contract you have with the person you are living with makes all the difference in terms of how protected your wealth and you are should you split up. Without a doubt, having a written cohabitation agreement is your best option. Without a contract, a court is more likely to order some kind of property division if

- your relationship lasted for "some time" (states vary quite a bit in this regard) and you lived together continuously;
- you pooled your resources for joint projects such as buying property or investing in a business—and you have the records to prove it; and
- your oral or implied contract looks like a straightforward "business" arrangement—that is, there was a clear exchange of services (e.g., I work for free in your practice, and you give me an interest in ownership in the business).

If you are thinking of moving in with someone or already do so and don't have a written contract, I urge you to get one. But what if that ship has sailed? What if you are living with someone without a written agreement and are thinking of separating or have already done so? What then?

RECOVERING MONEY OR PROPERTY WITHOUT A CONTRACT

If you are like many women who live with their partners, you have likely contributed to your partner's wealth either by working in his businesses without pay (e.g., doing the accounting in the evenings or serving as a receptionist on weekends) or by taking on the housekeeping and child-rearing work so your partner can focus on his business. If you split up and have no written or express oral contract between you, one way to get "paid back" for that contribution is to bring a legal claim against your former partner using the following three "legal theories," or principles based on the idea that the law should step in to prevent serious injustice: constructive trust, "quantum meruit," and unjust enrichment. These three legal theories might be used successfully in court, but they each pose challenges.

Constructive Trust

Constructive trust refers to a situation where someone has taken possession of property that belongs rightfully to you and a court makes them give it back; in essence, the court is saying that because the property rightfully belongs to you, the other person only possesses it "in trust" for you—that is, as a sort of custodian. When asking a court to apply a constructive trust theory, you are asking it to give you a share of property or assets to which you contributed and which you believe your partner should not, in fairness, keep all to himself.

Sandra and Kurt met in California in 1985 and formed what Sandra called a "a strong personal relationship."[11] Three years later, Kurt moved to San Jose and asked Sandra to move with him—in fact, she said, he asked her to quit her job, move, and marry him, and he promised to share everything with her and take care of her for the rest of her life. In return, he proposed she be his full-time domestic partner, housekeeper, and business partner, helping him to manage his rental properties as well as the home. Finally, in 1991, Sandra agreed, quit her job, and moved to San Jose, where she fulfilled all of the roles Kurt had asked of her, acting as a "cook, grocer, decorator, chauffeur, and nurse, hostess, and interior decorator; and professional services as leasing agent, cleaning contractor, and general contractor for [Kurt]'s portfolio of real estate, which increased in value partly as a result of her services." Kurt introduced her to others as his wife; they took the same last name.

Then, in 2001, Kurt decided he wanted out. He offered Sandra a check for $750 and suggested she move in with her son. Shocked, Sandra stayed and tried to repair the relationship (also, keep in mind, she didn't really have anywhere to go). But Kurt wasn't having it—he became verbally abusive to the point where she finally fled their home. When Sandra sued for the value of her labor for those ten years, Kurt testified that she had merely been a "guest" in his house all that time (apparently a guest who did housework and helped run his businesses). The court refused to grant Sandra relief, saying she had never expected to be paid for her services in the first place. (This issue comes up a lot in these cases, by the way. It makes sense: if you think you're building a life together, you don't expect to get an hourly wage. That doesn't mean you don't deserve compensation if that life doesn't materialize. So word to the wise: get something in writing and keep track of your work.)

Asking the courts to impose a constructive trust, however, doesn't always work. Technically, for a court to apply a theory of constructive trust, you'll need to show some kind of fraud or wrongdoing on the part of your partner. If you can't, some courts will refuse to do it.

Take the case of Lori and David,[12] who began an affair when she was fourteen and he was twenty-three. (I know what you're thinking: statutory rape, right? Well, yes. For some reason, no one went there. Have I told you to stay out of Mississippi?) Two years later, they moved in together and continued to live together for the next twelve years. During that time, they had two children; Lori did all the housework and childcare, and she managed a restaurant David owned. Witnesses at trial testified that Lori was always at the restaurant while David rarely was; she did all the ordering of supplies, hiring and firing of employees, and bookkeeping. For this she earned $250 a week—which she used to buy gas, groceries, and other items for their household, such as new carpeting, furniture, insurance, clothes for the children, and utility bills. They discussed marriage, but David never followed through.

They broke up on 2001. Lori asked for an equitable division of the property—again, that means that she acknowledged there was no contract but argued it would be unfair anyway for David to keep all the property, given how much work she put into making it profitable. The court, however, denied her request, getting very sniffy about the fact that they had never married. For a court to order a division of property, the court insisted, there had to be a ceremony of marriage—bright-line rule.

The court even ignored the fact that Lori had been fourteen at the beginning of the relationship and sixteen when they began living—and having children—together. It said the state had no interest in protecting her because she had waited until she was a legal adult—twenty-seven—to file the case. So she left David with all the benefits of her twelve years of household and management services and walked away with nothing.

This is an extreme case. But it shows the lengths some courts will go to in order to avoid fair compensation between cohabitants.

Quantum Meruit

Quantum meruit (Latin for "as much as he deserved")[13] is a legal theory that basically means you should get paid for what your labor was worth, even though you didn't for some reason get compensation for that labor at the time you did it. Courts, however, are reluctant to apply quantum meruit for three main reasons. First, you must show that you expected to be paid for your work at the time you did it and that the other person expected to pay for it. But as I mentioned earlier, the problem is that you probably *didn't* expect to be paid at the time; you were probably thinking of your labor not in monetary terms but rather as a contribution to the family life and financial future you were building together.

Second, courts tend to assume that housekeeping and other domestic work is done out of "love and affection" and not with an expectation of pay. (I know. Don't get me started.) So even if you did think of your labor in monetary terms, it will be hard to convince a court of that.

Third, even if the courts do apply quantum meruit, they will subtract from the value of the services you provided—cleaning, cooking, working in your partner's business, and so forth—the value of the support you received during that time. So, if you lived in a nice house, ate at nice restaurants, and took nice vacations during the relationship, the law will subtract whatever it thinks those things are worth from whatever you claim as the value of your services.

Unjust Enrichment

Unjust enrichment is similar to quantum meruit—it basically means that one person got wealthy at the other person's expense and owes them some kind of restitution. Bringing a claim of unjust enrichment when dividing property renders very unpredictable results. All depends on the particular facts of your situation and the biases of the particular court.

Joanne and Edward's story is a case in point. Joanne and Edward lived together for fourteen years. [14] Early on in the relationship, Edward bought a restaurant. Joanne cosigned the business loans and worked long hours in the restaurant. In the early days of the business, sometimes she got paid and other times she did not—it all depended on how the business was doing. The restaurant's profits were deposited into a joint account that both Edward and Joanne used.

A year or two into running the business, Edward asked Joanne to stop collecting pay for her work in the restaurant to increase his profits, and she agreed. Several years later, the couple split up. By then Edward's restaurant was turning a good profit and had increased in value. Joanne asked a court to compensate her for the unpaid hours she had put into the restaurant, claiming her free labor had allowed Edward to increase his wealth at her expense.

The court, however, said she could not be compensated for her work because that work, done in the context of a relationship, was presumed to be free, that it was no more than a girlfriend assisting her boyfriend in his business. Of course Joanne couldn't show that she had expected to be paid at the time, nor that Edward had expected to pay her—she thought they were securing their financial future together. That doesn't change the fact that when they broke up, Edward walked away with more wealth because of Joanne's free labor.

Or how about not just building a life together but also literally building a house to live that life in? Nina and Theodore started dating in 1998.[15] In 2000, they began to travel to Vermont on weekends, where Theodore owned a parcel of land, to prepare the land for building a house—that is, by uprooting trees, doing whatever grading of the ground, and staking the house location. In 2003, Theodore moved there to live full time; in 2005, Nina sold her house in Connecticut and joined him. Together they worked on finishing the house they were living in, with Theodore hiring contractors to do work they couldn't do. They shared expenses, including real estate taxes, insurance, and household bills. In 2012, Theodore decided it was over and asked Nina to leave.

Nina moved back to Connecticut and sued for compensation for the work she had done on the property, claiming that Theodore had been "unjustly enriched" by her uncompensated work on the house in which he now lived. She estimated her work on the house to be worth $330,000. Sound like a lot? Maybe. But imagine her situation: she had spent the past seven years working on a house she planned to live in with him, maybe for as long as she could foresee. Then, because the house is titled in his name, he can kick her out and go on living there, benefiting from all of her labor. It must have at least felt it was worth that much. And it was certainly worth more than nothing.

The court denied Nina's request for any compensation at all. It said she hadn't proved that Theodore had ever promised to pay her for the work (of course he hadn't!) and that all her labor was "incidental to the relationship" (in other words, she did it for love—which means no pay!). Of course it was "incidental to the relationship"—as long as there was one. After it ended, things were different: now it looked as if Nina had put years of free labor and love into a house she wasn't going to get to live in. Maybe she didn't deserve $330,000, but she did deserve something.

Here's another example of these "fairness" remedies failing: Linda and Don lived together for fourteen years and had a child together.[16] When they first moved in together, they agreed that they would pool their resources and earnings to build a life together. When their child was born, they agreed that Linda would stay home with her and Don would provide all their living expenses until the child was old enough for school. Linda left her job, stayed home, raised their child, and lost about five years of career advancement, income, and pension investment. During this time, Don bought two houses in succession, in which the couple and their child lived, and which Linda made improvements on while she was at home. Don sold both houses for a profit, which he kept as his separate property. After they had been together fourteen years, Don moved out. Linda wanted half the property, asserting that she had lost years of career, had kept house for Don so he could advance his businesses, had contributed to the profit made on the houses, and had made her sacrifices in reliance on her belief that they were building a permanent life together. The court disagreed, holding that she had no right to the profits made on the houses and refusing to find any kind of enforceable agreement between them because they were not legally married.

The central problem is that in intimate relationships, the promises are usually implied. As I keep saying, you should have a contract to protect yourself, but it's understandable that people don't in these situations. More often, the parties—or maybe one of them—assume they are in a permanent relationship based on all the components of their interactions. This is very human. To make property division depend on a piece of paper—rather than the substance of the relationship—seems silly and unfair. But it happens all the time.

If you end the relationship with your live-in partner and don't have a contract, it's unlikely that a court will help you recover money for work you might have done, time you have put in, or career opportunities that you have given up in the belief that you were securing a financial future together. If you've made sacrifices that benefited your partner and increased his wealth or earning potential, you might be left with nothing—no assets and a diminished ability to earn a living on your own. What many women who live with their partners don't realize is that they might end up in a similar financial bind if their partners die.

TILL DEATH DO US PART

The death of a partner or spouse can be one of the most stressful events a woman might experience in her lifetime. Not only do women have to process emotionally the grief of losing the person with whom they were sharing their lives, but also they have to deal with a daunting thicket of legal and financial matters. Sometimes couples have prepared for this event: they've left wills or trusts in place that spell out how their assets will be divided in the event one of them dies and have set up life insurance policies with each other named as the beneficiaries.

Unfortunately, most people do not. That leaves the vulnerable party—typically the woman in a heterosexual relationship—in a precarious position.

In a marriage, if your spouse dies, the law steps in to offer you some protection. If there's no will, or if a spouse is left out of a will, the law guarantees you a share of the other person's estate. But if you are just living together and your partner dies, you have no such protection. Without a will, you have no right to that person's estate. And if the person dies with a will that leaves you with little or nothing at all, you have few recourses to claim wealth that you have likely helped create or were promised.

That's precisely what happened to Eleanor. Eleanor had been dating Walter for about five years when he had a heart attack that left him unable to take care of himself.[17] He asked her to move in with him at his ranch outside of Sheridan, Wyoming. For thirteen years, Eleanor cared for Walter and his ranch.

"If he had to take a bath, I took him and gave him a bath. If he shaved, I had to shave him. He chose not to unless I did it for him,"[18] Eleanor told a court after Walter's death. She even cleaned up after Walter when he lost control of his bladder and bowels, and she managed all his medical care, getting his prescriptions, preparing his shots, and taking him to the VA hospital for his appointments. Eleanor also cooked all his meals, bought and washed his clothes, cleaned, kept the garden, and even painted his house.

At Walter's ranch, Eleanor worked hard together with her children and grandchildren to keep it going. "I took total care of all stock. I had to feed, water, and pull them in from the pasture. I did the baling. I drove his tractor," Eleanor explained. "Essentially, anything that needed to be done that he did not feel—or feel up to at that point, I did."[19]

In return for all this work, Walter promised Eleanor that he would leave her the ranch when he died. But at the time Walter passed away in 1992, his will contained only one paragraph: "I give, bequeath and devise, to my friend, Elly Adkins, ten (10) cows of her choosing from the cattle I own at the time of my death."

Because Walter's will did not spell out what would happen to his entire estate, the ranch and all his remaining assets passed under state law to members of his family. If Eleanor and Walter had been married, those same state laws would have ensured Eleanor a part of his estate. But because they just lived together, she got nothing more than ten cows.

Eleanor brought suit, claiming Walter's estate should reimburse her for all the services she had provided—to him, his ranch, and businesses—during his life and that Walter had promised to compensate her for these services anyway. But she made a big mistake. She admitted at trial that she performed all the services for Walter because she loved him. The court ruled that Eleanor acted out of love and affection—not because she expected to be paid—and that therefore Walter had no reason to compensate her.

The lesson in Eleanor's story is clear: even if your partner promises to leave you his assets when he dies, you have no recourse if he fails to do so—even if, like Eleanor, you took care of him when he was sick or performed other services for him that a stranger would have been paid for.

Finally, there's one other way in which the law fails to protect the vulnerable party—typically women—in the event their live-in partner dies: unlike married couples, in many states people who cohabit cannot sue for damages in the wrongful death of the other. The financial implications are significant when the partner who is killed is the breadwinner in the relationship: a judgment in the survivor's favor could make up for some of the loss of financial security for the dependent partner.

Police officers shot Valencia's boyfriend, Benson, with whom she lived, four times.[20] She heard the whole encounter from a neighbor's house, heard the shots, and heard him fall to the ground and cry out; he later died. She sued for recovery for emotional damages from seeing a loved one killed and losing his companionship but was barred from recovering: the law that allowed married partners to recover for damages for loss of spouses did not apply to couples who only lived together. It didn't matter that Valencia and Benson lived together, had a committed relationship, and depended on each other. Had they been legally married, Valencia could have sued for damages for the loss of his companionship, her emotional distress at his death, and the loss of his lifetime of earnings. Because they were not married, however, she could not sue for any kind of compensation. As more and more couples live together in relationships that are just as long term and committed as marriage, these laws seem archaic and unfair. But they remain the rule in many states.

STATES ARE DIFFERENT

As I keep saying, states vary greatly with respect to how they treat cohabitants upon separation. At one end of the spectrum is the state of Washington, which has a "Committed Intimate Relationship Statute."[21] This law creates a legal basis for division of property between unmarried cohabitants when the relationship ends. It is very similar to the laws providing for property division upon divorce, except that it applies only to property acquired during the relationship. Courts applying the statute look at the duration and purpose of the relationship, as well as whether the couple pooled resources and labor for joint projects.

At the other end of the spectrum, there are states like Mississippi, West Virginia, Ohio, New Mexico, and others that, as I've shown, make it very hard for you to receive compensation or property division if you just lived with someone without getting married—even if you gave up your career and helped him build up his business or the value of his property. In the next section, I look at business partnerships and how they are treated quite differently by the law, even though they look very similar.

COMPARE TO BUSINESS PARTNERSHIPS

It's interesting to compare the law between partners and spouses to comparable situations in commercial law, as I do throughout this book. It's interesting because there's always a similar situation in the commercial/business context that the law often treats quite differently—and often more fairly.

For example, marriage is a partnership, right? How does the law of business partnerships treat a partner who brings fewer or no assets to the partnership but who puts in more unpaid labor? That seems pretty analogous to some of our cohabitation stories, doesn't it? Isn't the stay-at-home partner with less wealth a lot like a partner who goes into business with a wealthier person who supplies the funds and equipment?

Well, yes. So can we look to partnership law for some helpful comparisons? I think the answer is yes, but I'm going to hold off this discussion until the chapter on divorce. For purposes of property distribution, cohabitation and marriage should be treated the same—as partnerships. When either one breaks up, it's like a business partnership ending, so I'm going to explain that analogy in detail in the later chapter on divorce. But keep it in mind.

PROTECT YOURSELF

But I still want to offer you suggestions for how to protect yourself in case your cohabitation breaks up. If you are living with someone, what can you do now to protect yourself in the event your partner dies? For starters, make sure your partner has a life insurance policy with you named as the beneficiary. This will at least ensure that if he dies, you will be able to replace, to some degree, the stream of income he had contributed to the relationship and your lifestyle when he was alive.

Equally important, talk with your partner about how you both want to share your assets when you die, and write wills stating clearly what you are leaving each other. Of course, you can't compel someone to write a will. So, if you and your partner decide to draft a cohabitation contract, include in it your agreement to leave your assets to the other person in your wills. Contracts that state you will put certain things in your will are valid in most states, but they must meet certain requirements.

I hope by now it's clear: contracts are incredibly important to protect yourself and the wealth that you've helped to create. So let's take a closer look at how to draft one that will stand up legally.

SETTING UP A SOLID CONTRACT

Throughout this chapter, I've been repeating over and over that if you are living with someone in a committed, intimate relationship, you must protect yourself by having a legally valid contract that spells out what will happen financially if you break up or one of you dies. But here I'll admit that, well, not *everyone* who is cohabiting needs one. If you have a well-established career, you are financially independent, and are financially stable—for example, you feel you are in good shape for your retirement—you may not need a cohabitation contract, especially if you and your partner have agreed to keep your assets such as bank accounts separate.

But if you answer yes to at least two or more of the following questions, you need a written contract:

- Are you living with someone in an intimate relationship that you think might lead to marriage?
- Do you have significantly fewer assets than your partner?
- If you work, do you earn less than your partner?
- Do you do the bulk of the housework and, if applicable, childcare?
- Did you give up educational or career opportunities to spend more time taking care of the home so your partner could focus on getting a degree or building a business?
- Did you make these decisions—to forego education or career advancement—relying on the fact that the two of you are building a life together?

Unfortunately, many women will answer yes to at least two of these questions. If that's you, get that contract.

Whenever possible, hire a lawyer to draft a cohabitation agreement and a will. Doing so is always the best course since a lawyer will know the ins and outs of your state's cohabitation laws and can anticipate issues you may not have thought of. And it might not be as expensive as you think.

If you can't afford a lawyer to draft your contract from scratch—or prefer to do it yourself—you can draft one yourself by following the guidelines below. The key to remember: your contract must show that there is an exchange of value—and that value can't be anything to do with sex, love, or affection (or even sound as if it is)!

For your contract to be legally binding, it will need to cover the following:

1. Spell Out What Each of You Is Giving in Exchange for This Agreement

To show there is an enforceable contract between you, it must state the date the two of you began living together and set out what each party is giving in exchange for the agreement. If one partner agrees to support the other, what is the other partner giving in exchange? It's very important that this not look like a contract for sexual services: courts will not enforce anything that looks like this kind of exchange. Housekeeping and childcare services, however, are valid forms of payment.

2. Make Full Disclosure of All Assets and Liabilities

The contract should disclose what each person owns and what each person's debt is. The purpose of disclosing assets and liabilities is to make sure you have made the agreement with full knowledge of your partner's assets, and therefore you have full knowledge of the relevant facts. This makes the contract valid. In some states, a contract can be set aside if there is inadequate disclosure of assets.

3. Detail How Expenses Will Be Shared While You Are Living Together

The contract should spell out who will pay what expenses while the two of you live together. Questions this section should address include the following:

- Will you have joint or separate bank accounts?
- Who will pay for household expenses, and who will be responsible for other routine and nonroutine expenses, such as insurance, home repairs, and so forth?
- Will you pool your income? If so, how? Will you split expenses equally, or will each person contribute to expenses in proportion to that person's income?

- Who will own new purchases—a car, a boat, or a house—particularly those paid for from pooled assets?
- If one person pays for maintenance or improvements to the other's property, how will that be treated? Will it give the paying person an interest in the property, or will it be considered a loan or a gift? If such payments are treated as a loan, will the loan be with interest?
- How will expenses be handled differently if one person loses his or her job or becomes ill or disabled?

4. State How Assets (Joint and Separate) Will Be Handled If You Break Up

The contract should state what each person wants the other to get if the relationship ends or if one person dies while you are still together. Remember that states do not make any provisions to support cohabitants who live together or to allow them to inherit from each other without a will. This agreement, however, can. Questions this section should address include the following:

- How will you define termination of the relationship? Two possibilities are when one person gives notice in writing to the other person and when one person moves out of the shared home.
- How will you divide jointly owned and commingled property? Will you sell it and share the money? Can you agree on a fair division?
- Will one of you provide the other with financial support after you end your relationship? How much? For how long? Does that person have adequate insurance (disability, long-term care, and life) to ensure that support can continue for as long as the contract dictates?
- What events would cause the termination of the support?
- Who will get the kids and the pets? (Agreements about child custody will not be enforced, but the agreement of the par-

ties may still carry some weight with the court, so it's worth thinking about custody, parenting, and so on in the event of a breakup. You can certainly create enforceable provisions for the custody and care of pets in your contract.)

- If one partner dies during the relationship, who will pay his or her debts?

5. Include the Following Additional Legal Provisions

Your agreement should also state the following:

- The agreement is binding (I know, duh, but trust me).
- Both parties promise to act in good faith—this means you promise to treat each other honestly and fairly over the course of the agreement.
- What is set forth in the document is the entire agreement— there are no other parts of the agreement written elsewhere.
- Both parties entered into the agreement of their own free will.
- Both parties either had an attorney or had the opportunity to have one and chose not to.
- The parties agree to execute any additional documents necessary to carry out the agreement, such as life insurance, bank accounts, and wills.
- The circumstances under which the agreement can be changed or terminated

In this chapter, I've shown you that the law in many states leaves couples who live together high and dry—and leaves the financially dependent partner especially vulnerable in a way a married spouse would not be. While there's really nothing you can do about the law, you can protect yourself by having a solid cohabitation contract in place. By the way, should you eventually decide to get married, drafting a cohabitation contract with your partner might turn out to be good practice for when you draft a prenuptial agreement.

2

THE TRUTH ABOUT
PRENUPTIAL AGREEMENTS

Susan was seventeen years old and still living with her parents, attending high school, and working part time in a ski shop when she met Louis who was forty-five.[1] After dating for two years, during which time Susan fought with her parents about the relationship and moved out into an apartment Louis paid for, Louis proposed. He gave her a beautiful diamond engagement ring. Before the wedding, Louis asked Susan to sign a prenuptial agreement, or prenup, telling her it was a "standard form" and advising her to get legal advice. The prenup stated that in case of divorce, each person would keep their separate assets and Susan would be entitled to $3,500 per year of the marriage, one year of health insurance, and a car. Since disclosure of each party's assets (or a waiver of disclosure) is required for an enforceable prenup, Louis prepared a list of his own assets and another list of Susan's. He stated the value of the engagement ring as $21,000, which meant Susan's assets, including the ring, totaled about $46,000. Louis's assets added up to more than three million.

Ten years later, the two separated, and Susan took the ring to a jeweler who told her it was in fact not a diamond but cubic zirconium—essentially worthless. Susan sued to invalidate the prenuptial agreement on the grounds that Louis fraudulently induced her to sign it and that he violated the duty of full and fair disclosure in the agreement by lying about the value of the engagement ring. The trial court agreed with Susan and invalidated the agreement. But the Supreme Court of Pennsylvania reversed, holding the prenuptial agreement valid because, it ruled, it was up to Susan to get the ring appraised at the time Louis gave it to her. It said that her failure to do so was "simply unreasonable." That is, trusting her fiancé—whom she had dated for two years and who was more than twenty-five years older than she was—not to lie to her and not to declare false information in a legal contract was beyond the bounds of reason.

Most people think that prenuptial or premarital agreements are only for celebrities and the very wealthy. But prenups, as they are commonly referred to, are on the rise—and not just among people who are remarrying or marrying late in life when both spouses might have significant assets of their own. While in those situations prenups can be helpful in protecting each person's assets, these agreements can also offer an excellent example of how laws that technically treat both spouses equally actually end up discriminating against the more vulnerable party—statistically likely to be the woman. In the past, courts refused to enforce these agreements: a husband could not do away with his duty to support his wife by having her sign a contract. Today, however, the law considers both spouses free to make whatever contract they wish and usually plays little or no role in assessing the fairness of the contract.

But this hands-off approach ignores the reality that many women are still not equal to men in many areas that affect their bargaining power: wealth, income, and career opportunities. A common situation involving prenups brings together an older, well-off man with a younger woman who has few assets and limited career potential. And yet, even if she felt cornered—she was pregnant when she signed the agreement, the partner threatened to call off the wedding, she had left a job or moved far from home in preparation for the upcoming marriage, or even if she had much less financial sophistication than her future spouse or had no genuine legal representation of her own to represent her in negotiations—most courts will enforce the prenup. The result is that women often sign prenups that later deprive them unjustly of wealth they helped create.

In this chapter, I explore how, by ignoring the inequalities between the parties in prenuptial agreements, the law reinforces the wealth gap between men and women. By sharing the stories of women who suffered significant losses as a result of prenups, I'll show you how difficult they are to get out of. My hope is that by the end of the chapter, you'll have a clear understanding of why these agreements should never be entered into lightly and what you can do if asked to sign one.

WHAT ARE PRENUPS AND WHY WOULD ANYONE SIGN ONE?

Prenuptial or premarital agreements are contracts between the spouses-to-be addressing a wide range of issues, but most often, they set out how property will be divided in case of divorce and what kind of support the financially dependent partner will receive. Prenups can be a useful tool for couples as they prepare to join their lives and build a future together. If you and your partner are entering into marriage with each having significant assets of your own, such as high-paying careers or children from a previous marriage you want to provide for, a prenup can help both of you protect your assets and achieve your goals. Even if there's disparity between your income or between your financial situation and your partner's, a prenup agreement that gives balanced consideration to both parties' interests and treats both fairly can benefit everyone. By stating upfront how your finances and assets will be dealt with if the unexpected happens—you get divorced—you might save a lot of conflict and money down the line.

The trouble arises when the prenup does not treat both parties fairly but rather is set up to protect the financial interests of one spouse exclusively by leaving the financially vulnerable or dependent spouse out in the cold. A typical scenario includes a financial-ly dependent woman whose fiancé is wealthier, has a more lucra-tive career or advanced degrees, or is older. The fiancé wants to protect his assets from the soon-to-be-spouse in case of divorce and prevent her from getting property and maybe even support that she would otherwise be entitled to under state law. He may also want to leave all his assets to his children from a prior mar-riage.

You may be asking yourself, why would a woman sign a prenup that leaves her without money or financial support if she divorces? The first reason is optimism bias, a common phenomenon where people believe they are less likely to experience an adverse event than other people. Despite the reality that half of marriages end in divorce, no one thinks it will happen to them. They especially don't when they are head-over-heels in love with someone—and in the throes of planning a wedding, which is often when the fiancé demands that the bride-to-be sign the prenup.

Second, women tend to trust their prospective spouses to have their best interests at heart. After all, they are in love. These wom-en assume their fiancés would never harm them financially if the relationship were to end. As we'll see later, this is often not the case.

And finally, I believe that while we may have come a long way in terms of career advancement and financial independence, women are still targeted by countless subliminal, cultural mes-sages via advertisements, TV shows, and more that tell us to give relationships and marriage more importance than men do. So when your fiancé whips out a prenup shortly before your wedding and tells you to sign it or the wedding is off, it may have a pro-found emotional effect on you. You may feel too embarrassed at the thought of calling off the wedding, you may worry people will think you're a failure, or you may fear losing the wonderful life—a marriage, family, and kids—you've been dreaming about.

For these reasons, many women sign prenup agreements with-out legal advice from a lawyer to represent them (by which I do not mean their fiancé's lawyer or one he refers her to), or even after a lawyer who has reviewed it tells them *not* to sign it. Now, it's easy to judge them and believe you would never do the same— you would never make such a bad decision (that optimism bias again!). But when you are so deeply in love that you cannot conceive of your fiancé not having your best interests in mind or you feel you've been emotionally blindsided, it's hard to remain cool about legal and financial matters. The truth is, many smart women have signed prenups that hurt them. And you can't be sure that in a similar situation you wouldn't do the same. The best way to prevent that from happening (or if you've already signed a prenup, to be aware of its consequences) is to learn more about why prenups often hurt women.

ONCE SIGNED, THERE'S NO WAY OUT

The reason prenups are powerful tools for making financial arrangements before getting married is also the reason they should never be entered into lightly: prenup agreements trump state law. For example, in most states if you divorce you might be entitled to property division, spousal support, and maybe to having your attorney's fees covered. Or if your spouse dies without a will or leaves you out of the will, the laws of your state probably guarantee you as a surviving spouse a share of the dead spouse's estate. But if you sign a prenup that waives these rights away, the agreement will supersede those state laws. Once you've signed it, it's very, very hard—almost impossible in some states—to get out of it.

You might still think you can get out of the prenup, for example, if you signed it under duress, if there's been a significant change in circumstances such as one spouse's wealth increases drastically, if your marriage lasted a very long time, or if your spouse lied to you about his assets when signing the prenup. Wrong. Courts rarely invalidate prenups. Even if you go to trial to get your prenup invalidated and a court agrees with you, the appeals court is very likely to reverse that judgment. Understanding how trial and appeals courts work and hearing cases might help explain why.

The trial court is the first time you take your case in front of a judge and maybe also a jury. These judges and juries see and hear testimony from the parties involved—the husband and wife, and possibly other witnesses. As a result, they often develop empathy for the vulnerable party. The appeals court judges, however, don't hear from the parties directly. They just hear from their lawyers— sometimes only in written form. Under those circumstances, it's easier for them to miss the human side of the case or to truly grasp the dependent party's vulnerability. For that reason, appeals courts tend to look at the law separate from the human reality of the case. The problem, as I've explained earlier in the book, is that if you look at the law in isolation, it seems to treat everyone fairly and equally. It's only when you see the actual circumstances of the people involved that you see how unfair it can be.

(It's worth noting that this pattern—the trial court often rules for the vulnerable party and the appeals court reverses in support of the other spouse—is one that tends to favor the person with the resources to pay for the appeal: too often, the husband.)

The bottom line: getting out of a prenup agreement is extremely unlikely, regardless of your circumstances. Here are some reasons you might think an unfair prenup would be invalidated by the courts—and an explanation for why the courts (many of them appeals courts) chose to enforce them instead.

You Sign under "Duress"

Normally, if you sign a contract under duress, the contract is not valid. When someone is pressuring or coercing you into doing something you wouldn't normally do, that's duress. The law defines duress as a "lack of a meaningful choice," that is, the other person leaves you with no reasonable alternative but to do what they want you to do. For example, your insurance company tells you to agree to higher rates or it will cut off coverage immediately.

Your choice is agree to the rates or lose your insurance right away—not a meaningful choice. According to the law, duress doesn't need to involve physical force. In fact, the law specifically recognizes "emotional duress," which doesn't involve a physical threat. Many women sign prenup agreements under what many would consider emotional duress. But courts rarely agree.

Mary Anne began a long-distance relationship with James while she was living in Arlington, Virginia, and working as a consultant.[2] James lived in Charleston, West Virginia, where he owned an accounting firm. In 1995, Mary Anne discovered she was pregnant so they got engaged. She quit her job and moved to Charleston to start a married life with James. Shortly before the wedding day, James asked Mary Anne to sign a prenup. He had many more assets than Mary Ann, so he wanted to keep their property separate and for her to waive any claim to support in the event of divorce. If she didn't sign, he said, he wouldn't marry her.

Mary Anne sought the advice of a lawyer who negotiated the prenup on her behalf with James's lawyer. Mary Anne's lawyer, in fact, did get some revisions in the contract that benefited her: specifically, James agreed to fund an annuity for Mary Anne during the marriage. By the time Mary Anne saw the revised agreement, it was only a few days before the wedding. At this point, she was seven months' pregnant and had no job, no insurance, and no place to live. When James repeated that he would not marry her unless she signed it, she gave in and did.

During the marriage, James formed a second accounting firm and bought several businesses and rental properties. Mary Anne, at his request, stayed home, raised their child, and did all the housekeeping. By 2009, the marriage was on the rocks and Mary Anne filed for divorce on grounds of adultery, among other things.

Under the prenup, she could get no share of the businesses acquired during the marriage because they were James's separate property. But Mary Anne argued that she was under duress when she signed the agreement. Pregnant, and without health insurance or a place to live, she felt she had no choice but to accept James's prenup. She also argued that the agreement was unfair because it gave James the full value of her childcare and homemaking services (which freed him to build his wealth) for all the years they were married while she got nothing in return to keep once the marriage broke up. Finally, she pointed out that James had breached his one obligation under the agreement—the promise to fund an annuity for her during the marriage.

The court, however, disagreed. It first noted that the West Virginia legislature had passed a law that pregnancy could not be considered "duress" in signing a prenup. (You might be thinking, *wait, what?* Well, think about who's in the legislature.) As for James's breach of the contract, the court said "no harm done." James simply had to pay Mary Anne an amount equivalent to the payments he would have made had he set up an annuity. Of course, the way annuities work is that the initial payments are investments that get paid back to the payee later in periodic installments totaling a larger amount than the original payments. Just giving her the missed payments didn't really make up for what she lost. Had he made those payments, they would have earned income and ended up totaling a larger amount than what Mary Anne got. On the other hand, James got all the value of Mary Anne's housekeeping and childcare services all those years, which enabled him to go out and prosper in his business endeavors.

Many courts simply refuse to understand that pregnancy can amount to duress in the context of signing a prenup. Even in a state you might think was pretty enlightened, courts have this blind spot. Here's a Massachusetts case: When Mary and Tim began dating, she was a thirty-five-year-old home economics teacher with three kids from a former marriage; he was a thirty-one-year-old doctor.[3] He owned about a million in assets and earned $6,400 per week; Mary had about $100,000 in assets, and her weekly salary was $1,675. About a year into the relationship, Mary became pregnant. Later, at trial, she testified that Tim had insisted she become pregnant as a condition of marrying her: according to her, Tim wanted children and was worried that Mary's age—thirty-five!—would make it hard for her to get pregnant; he wanted to make sure of her fertility. (Not surprisingly, Tim "vigorously disputed" that there was any such agreement, and, maybe also not surprisingly, the judge believed him.) Anyway—when she told Tim she was pregnant, Tim suddenly added a new condition to the marriage: he insisted she sign a prenup waiving any claim to property division if they ever divorced.

Tim's lawyer drew up the prenup and showed it to Mary, who showed it to a lawyer who—you know what's coming, right?—told her not to sign it. But she did not try to negotiate the terms of the agreement. (Would you, in her position? Be honest.) When Tim, Tim's lawyer, and Mary met at a restaurant to go over the prenup, Mary kept breaking down and crying, saying she did not want to sign it. But after they left the restaurant, they drove to a bank, where she did sign it in front of a notary.

Can we pause and try to understand Mary's emotional state at this point? Are you rolling your eyes at her right now, thinking, *What the heck was the matter with her?* Her lawyer warned her not to sign it, she knew signing it was a bad idea, and she signed it anyway. Well, first, unlike the court, let's do her the credit of believing her: Tim tells her he wants to marry her but says he needs her to prove she could still get pregnant so they can have kids of their own. She already has three kids. She earns about $1,500 per week. She's pregnant, feeling vulnerable—she's well past the first trimester at this point—and she wants to marry Tim and have a child together; she loves him and is touched that he wants this same thing. What were her options at that point? Are her emotions understandable? Doesn't this situation amount to duress—the lack of reasonable alternatives? And are you really sure, deep down, that you wouldn't have done what she did?

So Tim and Mary did get married. They were married for ten years and had two children. During that time, they agreed that Mary would quit her job, raise their two children, and run the household. After ten years Tim filed for divorce and asked the court to hold the prenup enforceable. Mary argued that she had been under duress when she signed the prenup. The court disagreed.

So much for being able to get out of a prenup signed under duress.

Compare the Way Courts Treat Commercial Contracts

Just as in cohabitation, it's interesting to look at the way courts treat similar issues—duress, unfairness, and lack of meaningful choice—in commercial contracts. For example, here are the facts of a famous case establishing an important rule for unconscionable contracts: Mrs. Williams, mother of seven children with a limited education and not much money, bought several items of furniture from Walker Thomas Furniture in Washington, D.C.[4] Because she bought them on an installment plan, she had to sign several contracts—fourteen, to be precise—full of legalese in very fine print. In essence, the contracts said that if she fell behind on a payment, the store could repossess *all* the furniture, even if the total amount she had paid by that point was enough to cover some of the pieces. She bought $1,800 worth of furniture and paid off all but $164 and then bought a stereo for $514 and defaulted. The store repossessed all the furniture—as the contract stated. Represented by Legal Aid, Mrs. Williams sued.

The court said that the contract should be voided if it were found to be unconscionable—basically, extremely unfair—and defined this as when "a party of little bargaining power and hence little real choice, signs a commercially unreasonable contract with little or no knowledge of its terms."

This is the rule for finding a contract void. OK, so let's apply the rule to our prenup cases. "A party of little bargaining power with little real choice": how much bargaining power does a pregnant woman without a home, health insurance, or job—who got pregnant based on the assumption that she and her partner would build a life together—have? Mrs. Williams could have just walked away, right? No harm, no foul—she still had a home and a job, at least—and no baby who would now be born out of wedlock. Surely the pregnant woman has less bargaining power than Mrs. Williams did. *Little real choice?* Couldn't Mrs. Williams have lived without furniture more easily than Mary could have found a home and new job and raised her baby by herself?

By the way, I'm not defending the way the furniture store treated Mrs. Williams (and others like her), who in fact had very few options—she didn't have enough money to buy the pieces outright, she lived in a metro area and didn't have a car to drive out to the suburbs where such goods where cheaper, and most of the stores in her neighborhood were equally unscrupulous. I'm just pointing out how much easier it is for courts to see unfairness when it's an economic situation they can relate to, and showing you how unfair it is for the same standards not to apply to the cases of a prenup signed under the duress of pregnancy.

But let's look at the court's other requirements for unfairness— and remember, a court may invalidate a contract for egregious unfairness. The *Williams* court also notes that the contract was "commercially unreasonable" and that Mrs. Williams had "little or no knowledge of its terms." The court thought that the terms of the contract she signed were commercially unreasonable because they allowed the furniture company to repossess *all* of the furniture if Mrs. Williams fell behind on *any* payment, that is, it didn't allow her to keep the furniture she had in fact already paid for. This does seem ridiculously unfair, right? I agree. Most people would.

So how does this unfairness compare to a prenup that leaves a stay-at-home or part-time working wife who put in ten years of childcare, housekeeping, and support—with nothing but what she came with? That seems commercially unreasonable, doesn't it? In fact, the two situations seem similar: Mrs. Williams and the wife both lose everything they've invested because, well into the bargain, something goes wrong and the party with the bargaining power pulls out.

But maybe you're thinking there's one part of this I left out that might explain the difference between the two cases. The court did say that one ingredient of the contract's unfairness was that Mrs. Williams had "little or no knowledge of its terms." What about all those women who signed prenups knowing what they said, after their lawyers told them not to?

Well, here's a more recent case of an unfair commercial contract; let's see if that helps: Loral Corporation was a defense contractor who contracted with the navy to produce six million dollars' worth of radar sets.[5] The contract had some standard provisions such as delivery dates, a cancellation clause in case Loral failed to deliver, and a clause requiring Loral to pay damages if it delivered the sets late. Loral then hired Austin Instruments Corporation as a subcontractor to supply parts it needed to produce the sets.

All went well until Loral got a second contract for navy radar sets. It again asked for bids, and Austin again submitted bids. This time, however, Austin's bid was only competitive on some of the parts, and Loral told them it only wanted those parts on which its bid was the lowest. Austin refused this deal and insisted that Loral buy all the parts from them. Austin also threatened to stop delivering the parts it owed under the first contract if Loral didn't sign. Loral tried to find another manufacturer for the parts it needed but couldn't find one. Remember the first contract: if Loral failed to deliver, or delivered late, it would have to pay the navy substantial penalties. So Loral signed the new contract with Austin, on Austin's terms.

Let's pause here. Can we agree that Loral's lawyers knew what they were signing, that they understood the terms they were agreeing to? Safe bet, right? They just decided to agree to the unfair terms because they felt they had no choice: the downside of not agreeing would have cost them too much. After the contract was signed, Austin delivered the parts and Loral fulfilled its contract with the navy. Then Loral sued to recover the amount of the price increase it had paid Austin.

Again, hit pause. We've agreed that Loral certainly understood the terms of the contract they signed. Moreover, they got what they bargained for—Austin delivered the parts and Loral got paid for its contract with the navy. So what did the court say?

The court found that Austin had forced Loral to sign the contract by using duress and that it had to pay back all the extra money it had charged. It said there was duress because, first, Austin made a wrongful threat that made it impossible for Loral to exercise free will, and second, there was no other way for Loral to get the parts it needed.

Let's apply these criteria to our prenup situations. First, were the threats to call off the marriage "wrongful"? Notice that wrongful doesn't mean illegal—in the Loral case, Austin didn't do anything illegal. It just made a very immoral threat to breach a contract that left the other party with no alternatives. This is, in fact, the legal definition of a wrongful threat—and a wrongful threat in commercial law creates duress, which in turn could lead a court to void a contract. Isn't this what's happening in the prenup cases?

Think about Mary, the home economics teacher, and Tim, the doctor. She's thirty-five years old and earns about $1,500 a week. She already has three kids but gets pregnant to prove to Tim that they can have kids together once they are married. Then, at the last minute, he pulls out a prenup. She's crying as they meet with his lawyer to go over it, but she signs it anyway. Is this very different from the facts of Loral? I doubt that the Loral lawyers were crying when they signed the unfair contract with Austin (although they might have felt like it). But they felt they had no choice—and a court later agreed.

Or consider Mary Anne, who quit her job and moved to a strange city in a different state when she became pregnant, in preparation for married life with James, her fiancé. A few days before the wedding, when she was seven months' pregnant, she saw the final version of the prenup, which waived her right to any of James's property. Did she have any more choice in signing it than Loral had in signing the contract with Austin? The contract with Austin only involved money; Mary Anne's contract with James really put her life—and that of her baby—on the line. His threat to break off the engagement left her with no options—what was she supposed to do, look for alternate fiancés? So why do courts treat these cases so differently?

Well, here's a thought: backlash, anyone?

You Experience Drastic and Unforeseeable Changes in Circumstances

You might think that if you sign a prenup but your husband's or your circumstances change in some drastic, unforeseeable way later in the marriage—for example, one of you acquires significantly more wealth than expected or is disabled and cannot work—then a prenup would not be enforceable. Technically you'd be correct. The court does consider "drastic and unforeseeable" changes when deciding whether to void a prenup. But what's considered "drastic" and what's "unforeseeable"? In the context of prenups, your definition might be different from the law's.

Take the case of Catherine and Peter, who had been living together for four years when Catherine got pregnant.[6] While Catherine was waiting for her appointment at a clinic to terminate the pregnancy, Peter called her and begged her not to have the abortion. He asked her to marry him and raise the child together instead. Catherine agreed. A few days later—nine or ten days before the wedding—Peter presented Catherine with a prenup, telling her signing it was "just a formality" and promising her he would "always take care of her." (By the way, when someone tells you something is "just a formality," it's a sure sign that it's much more than that.)

At the time they signed the contract, Catherine had a high school education, a job as a restaurant hostess, and assets totaling about $10,000. Peter, meanwhile, had a college degree, owned his own business, and had a net worth around $5 million. The prenup stated that Peter's and Catherine's separate property would remain separate, staying with the owner in case of separation. The prenup also limited Catherine's support in case of divorce to $3,000 per month for only four years.

After eighteen years of marriage and four children, Peter filed for divorce and sought to enforce the prenup. Peter's net worth at this point was more than $22 million. Catherine argued that the $15 million increase in Peter's net worth was such a drastic change in circumstances that it would be unfair to enforce the prenup she had signed nearly twenty years before. But the court held that Peter's enormous increase in wealth over the course of the marriage was foreseeable at the time she signed the prenup, and therefore it would not be unfair to enforce it.

OK, so forget getting out of your prenup if there's been a drastic change in your spouse's net worth. But how about if you suffer a severe and unexpected illness? Would the court rule that a prenup is unenforceable then? Not in the case of Mary.

Mary met Jerry while she was the office manager at a law firm handling Jerry's second divorce (I know: that should have been a hint for Mary right there).[7] They started dating, and soon Mary moved in with Jerry. After about a year, Jerry proposed and they set a wedding date for the following year. Before the wedding, he gave her a prenup waiving her claims to alimony or property if they divorced. Mary showed the contract to the lawyer she worked for, who told her not to sign it. But Mary, although upset about the prenup, signed it anyway, and the couple were married. At the time of the marriage, Mary had diabetes and sponge kidneys, a birth defect in the kidney that impairs the flow of urine and can cause other problems such as urinary tract infections and kidney disease.

After six years of marriage, Mary found out Jerry was having an affair. She kicked him out of the house and filed for divorce on grounds of adultery, drunkenness, and physical cruelty. The trial court granted her divorce and decreed the prenup unenforceable because there had been a drastic change in circumstances since the signing, namely, Mary now had much more severe health problems such as neuropathy, lupus, heart irregularities, and vision and thyroid problems. She was now completely disabled and unable to work or support herself. The court awarded Mary permanent alimony and 30 percent of the property acquired during the marriage, noting that without the alimony she would likely depend on the state to support her.

Jerry appealed, arguing that the alimony provisions in the prenup should be enforced. The Supreme Court of South Carolina agreed with him, stating that it would be unfair to Jerry to invalidate an agreement signed by a party who was "fully aware of serious health issues and declining health." Interestingly, the court noted in a footnote (footnotes are often where courts tuck facts they want to ignore) that Mary suffered from new and unanticipated health problems and conditions that had arisen since she signed the prenup. But it also noted that Mary had gotten substantial benefits during the marriage in the form of a higher living standard, several houses, and luxury cars.

Of course, it's not much use to Mary that she had lived in fancy houses and driven luxury cars during the marriage. The point is that when she signed the prenup, Mary didn't anticipate having health issues so severe that she wouldn't be able to support herself in the event of divorce—and now finds herself in an incredibly precarious financial situation.

Your Spouse Manipulates Your Shared Wealth

Many women sign prenups agreeing to keep their assets separate from those of their spouses. They also agree to keep only their property in case of divorce but to share assets jointly acquired and income earned by separate property during the marriage. Now, what happens if you sign such an agreement and your spouse manipulates the finances to deplete your assets and accumulate more of his own? Would your spouse's underhanded dealings be grounds for invalidating the prenup? By now you can probably guess the answer. Even in this situation, the court won't necessarily help you get out of the agreement. Anita Kay is a case in point.

Anita married Harold in the state of Georgia when she was fifty-one years old and he was fifty-four.[8] At the time of the marriage, her assets were $37,000 and his were worth almost $1 million, including a jewelry business, a home, and several investment accounts. Before the wedding, they signed a prenup that stated they would share assets and income jointly acquired during the marriage.

While they were married, both Anita and Harold worked on Harold's jewelry business. But the entire time, Harold manipulated the books so there would be no apparent income from it—and therefore no "jointly acquired assets" from the marriage. For example, by not paying himself a salary, he made it look as if he wasn't earning an income (which would have been jointly acquired property subject to sharing with Anita). He also "borrowed" money from his brokerage accounts and then paid it back from the business funds—in larger amounts than he had borrowed. This way, he transformed potential "jointly acquired" property into his separate property. He also spent all of the money his wife inherited from her family during the marriage on improvements to his own property.

After thirteen years of marriage, Harold filed for divorce. By then, Anita had no assets of her own. She contested the prenup on the grounds that Harold's manipulation of the assets was a "changed circumstance" that made it unenforceable. While the trial court agreed, the court of appeals reversed, finding that Anita could have anticipated Harold's financial manipulation when she signed the prenup—therefore, it was not a changed circumstance. The court's ruling reflects a bizarre view of marriage and fairness: since Anita should have anticipated her spouse would cheat her while they were married, the prenup holds and Harold gets to keep the money that was rightfully hers.

There's no doubt that Anita should have been paying more attention to what Harold was doing with the money they earned from the business. Unfortunately, women all too often relegate the details of marital finances to their husbands. (Do you? Will you?) After all, most spouses—women especially—trust their partners to look out for their best interests. But is it fair for the court to blame the wife for *not expecting* her husband to cheat her and not actively looking out for his deception?

You Sign While Mentally Incapacitated or Disabled

If you think you might be able to get out of a prenup because you signed it while you were not fully in control of your mental capacity or have a developmental disability, think again. Mary's story, as well as the following one about Gita, show that in the context of a prenup, a contract signed by a mentally ill or disabled person who might not be able to give legal consent can still be enforceable.

Before marrying Joseph, Gita signed a prenup that waived both spouses' claims to inherit from whichever spouse died first.[9] Four years after the marriage, Joseph died. Per the inheritance laws of her state, Gita, as the surviving spouse, would have received a share of Joseph's estate. But since the prenup she signed superseded these laws, Joseph's family received his entire estate.

Gita, however, claimed the prenup was invalid because she was mentally ill and did not have the mental capacity to sign a legal contract. Gita had been diagnosed with bipolar disorder with severe psychotic features and, a few months before she signed the prenup, had been hospitalized for treatment. She was still receiving outpatient therapy when she signed the prenup. At the trial, a psychiatrist even testified that Gita had bipolar disorder and suffered from a thought-process disorder that prevented her from thinking logically and processing information. Not only did the psychiatrist testify that her judgment was impaired, but also Gita's lawyers produced medical records that included diagnoses of "delusional thinking," severely impaired judgment, and lack of impulse control—diagnoses made around the date she signed the prenup.

Nonetheless, the court declined to invalidate the prenup, saying her judgment at the time of signing was at least "fair." How did they come to this conclusion? They noted that she had held several jobs during the period in which she signed the agreement. Gita had worked half a year as a secretary, a year as a health care aide, and then as Joseph's assistant in his photography business. Although these brief stints of employment might otherwise raise a few red flags about Gita's ability to function, the court took them as signs of her legal capacity.

If a mentally ill person who, according the expert testimony, suffered from impaired judgment and was diagnosed as having "delusional thinking" was considered bound to her prenup, what chance do you have? Your chances are not very good even if you have a developmental disability. Mary's story proves that point.

Mary was developmentally disabled and unemployed—she qualified for and received Supplemental Security Income (a federal program that provides income for individuals with few financial resources and who have a physical or mental impairment that prevents them from working).[10] In high school, she had only attended special education classes. She did not even drive a car. When she was twenty-one years old, she married Lawrence who was sixty-two.

Two days before the wedding, Lawrence took Mary to see his attorney, who gave Mary a copy of a prenup he had prepared several weeks earlier and that waived Mary's claims to Lawrence's estate when he died. According to later trial transcripts, the attorney "discussed the pertinent parts of the agreement" with the two of them. The prenup listed Lawrence's property as "two adjoining parcels of real property, where he now resides, various items of logging equipment" as well as a boat and two cars. Mary's property consisted of "various personal effects, a bed, and two dressers." Mary, without the advice of independent counsel, signed the agreement.

After four years of marriage, Lawrence died. Per the prenup, Mary got nothing. So she contested the prenup, arguing that she was mentally disabled and unable to understand it when she signed. Despite noting that Mary had poor reading and writing skills and had never had a job, the court found the agreement was enforceable because there was no evidence that she did not understand it.

What's most troubling about Gita's and Mary's stories and those of other women who signed prenups under similar circumstances is that one can't even say that they made a bad decision:

it's simply not clear they were mentally capable of making a rational decision about signing any legal document at all. Their stories show just how far courts are willing to go to enforce prenup agreements.

Your Spouse Lies about His Assets

You would think the law might not look kindly on someone who lies and would invalidate any contract in which he falsely represented his assets. But when it comes to prenup agreements, you must understand that most courts will put the onus on you to verify the veracity of your soon-to-be-spouse's claim. The courts won't necessary care if your spouse lied or omitted information that might have led you to not sign the agreement. Take Victoria's story.

A British citizen with a high school education, Victoria met David, an American trader and investment manager, while working as his personal assistant at an investment firm in London.[11] A week after working for him, Victoria began dating David, and two months later, she moved in with him. Their arrangement was that David would pay the rent, while Victoria would pay her individual expenses. In 1997, Victoria moved to the United States to oversee the renovation and furnishing of a home David had bought in Westport, Connecticut. She traveled every three months back to England to satisfy the requirements of her tourist visa, emptying her savings in the process. After a year of traveling back and forth, Victoria was told she could not enter the United States again unless her immigration status changed. After consulting an immigration attorney who suggested they marry as a way to change her status, David proposed to Victoria—but insisted on a prenup as a prerequisite to marrying her.

Victoria wasn't familiar with the American concept of a prenup (at that time, they weren't enforceable in England), but she agreed to it because David wanted one. A few days before the ceremony, David showed Victoria a faxed version of the prenup and told her to get it signed. The agreement stated, among other things, that "each party acknowledges for himself or herself that both parties have substantial assets and that each would be able to adequately support himself or herself" in the case of divorce. Victoria's assets at this time totaled about $22,000, while David's were about $6 million, but these numbers were not on the faxed version of the prenup: there were blank spaces where the parties' incomes should have been filled in. The attached lists of assets were also blank.

David told Victoria to contact his sister-in-law, an attorney, who had an associate who would look over the prenup for her. This attorney met with Victoria for a half hour. But although he had received the complete list of David's assets, he didn't discuss it or the rest of the agreement with her. A day before the wedding, David and Victoria met in the attorney's office to sign the prenup. This time, the version of the agreement included a list of assets attached, which Victoria had a chance to review for the first time. After twenty minutes or so of looking over the list, she signed the prenup.

But here's the thing: the list of David's assets didn't clearly specify their values. For example, one of his assets was listed as "Ornstein Real Estate Venture" and listed its value as "85." Did that mean $85,000? Eighty-five million? Eighty-five what, exactly? All of David's assets were listed this way. There was no way for Victoria to assess what he was worth. In fact, it's a good bet that the whole rigmarole was a setup to get Victoria's signature on the agreement without her knowing what she was giving up.

After four years of marriage, Victoria filed for divorce. She claimed the prenup was unenforceable because there was a lack of financial disclosure and she didn't have a chance to consult with independent counsel. The trial court agreed with her, invalidated the prenup, and divided the property between them. David appealed, and you guessed it, the appeals court reversed.

According to the appeals court, Victoria's lack of financial knowledge and sophistication didn't matter. There had been adequate disclosure, the court said, because when she had been working for him she had at times submitted his expense accounts and copied his personal financial records for him, which should have made her aware of David's assets. In any case, this didn't matter because her attorney—the friend of David's sister-in-law—had the list of assets. True, he didn't show it to her until the day before the wedding, but that didn't matter because *anything an attorney knows it is assumed his client knows as well.* So the court decided that Victoria, in effect, knew what the list of assets included several weeks before she ever actually saw it.

What can we learn from Victoria's story? First, don't assume your partner wouldn't lie to you about his assets—or try to conceal them from you. Trust if you want, but in the famous words of Ronald Reagan, verify too. Second, courts don't care if your soon-to-be-spouse lied to you or got you to sign a prenup by withholding information. They will not void the prenup. They will expect you to have verified anything your fiancé claims in the prenup.

As with many other women profiled in this chapter, Victoria made some bad decisions: quitting her job, moving to another country without employment prospects, and not demanding an attorney of her own to explain the prenup and negotiate it on her behalf. And like many of these women, she was sheltered and naive about financial and legal matters. In some ways, we could argue that she contributed to the situation she found herself in. My point is not to defend her failure to stand up for herself but rather to show you that the law will cut you no slack at all after signing a prenup. I share her and the other women's cautionary tales in the hopes that should you find yourself in a similar position, they will inspire you to muster the courage to say, OK, call the wedding off. If you have signed a prenup agreement under similar circumstances, I hope the stories encourage you to discuss your specific situation with a lawyer right away.

OK, you signed it, but what if the prenup is just plain old unfair? Don't think a court will let you out of it.

Before she married Joseph, Susan lived with her daughter in a rented two-bedroom house; worked as a secretary, earning $25,000 a year; and owned no assets to speak of.[12] Joseph, on the other hand, owned a family construction business and had assets of more than one million. Each knew of the other's financial position. When they began to discuss marriage, Joseph made it clear from the beginning that he would insist on a prenup. Susan hired an attorney, who represented her in the negotiations. Ultimately, the agreement they signed represented mostly what Joseph wanted and made very little provision for Susan: if they divorced, she would get $35,000 a year, the marital home, medical insurance, and a car.

When they did divorce, after ten years of marriage, Susan admitted that, yes, she had signed the prenup, and yes, she had been represented by competent counsel, and yes, Joseph had fully disclosed his assets—but she argued nonetheless that it was simply unfair. While she had been financially dependent on Joseph for ten years, she was now left with almost nothing from the marriage except a house, a car, a very small yearly stipend, and medical insurance. In fact, the trial judge agreed with Susan, ruling that the agreement was unfair even at the time it was signed. But Joseph appealed—here we go again—and the appeals court agreed with him. It said that the prenup didn't leave Susan with nothing from the marriage—true—and that Susan had known what she was signing and had had a competent attorney. Therefore, it held that the agreement wasn't unfair.

You may agree with the appeals court; indeed, it's not crazy to do so: Susan did have an attorney, she knew what Joseph's assets were, and she agreed that she signed the contract willingly. Like you maybe, she never thought the marriage would end in divorce. But the lesson here is, you'll be held to what you sign, no matter how unfair it may be—don't delude yourself that you can "get out of it" later. And there may well be a later . . .

PROTECT YOURSELF

If you have signed a prenup agreement, there might not be much you can do at this point except understand its implications and shield yourself from the consequences as best as you can. For starters, become more involved in the family finances. For example, if you have waived your right to your husband's property if you divorce or when he dies—but not to joint property acquired during the marriage—make sure any property that is acquired during the marriage (say, your house) is titled under both your names.

If you are engaged and suspect—or expect—that your fiancé will ask you to sign a prenup agreement (or he's already demanded you do), these are some of the things you should do:

Postpone the wedding. Are you being pressured to sign the agreement a few days—or less—before the wedding? Drop the flower arrangements and find a lawyer. If he tells you the wedding is off if you don't sign, call his bluff. Maybe he'll be the embarrassed one—when everyone finds out why you postponed the wedding.

Get a lawyer of your own. Don't trust your fiancé's lawyer; he or she represents your fiancé, not you, whatever the law says. The two of you are "adverse" in this situation, which is legalese for "having opposing interests." One lawyer can't adequately represent both of you. If you can't afford a lawyer to negotiate on your behalf, at least hire a lawyer to look over the agreement. Even if you are broke, borrow money from someone if you need to. Hiring a lawyer may be costly, but if the lawyer is able to help you negotiate a fairer prenup, it might pay off at the end if you divorce (remember, fifty-fifty chance).

Find the right attorney. Look for a matrimonial attorney who is experienced in drafting and reviewing prenups. A good place to start is the American Academy of Matrimonial Lawyers (AAML). (Their website provides a list of attorneys in each state.) Only the most skilled and ethical lawyers are admitted to the AAML; if you choose someone from their local chapter, you are assured competent and responsible representation. And no, these attorneys are not necessarily the most expensive.

Read the prenup yourself. Make sure you understand the prenup agreement before you sign it. Highlight whatever you don't understand, and have your lawyer explain it to you. Pay particular attention whenever you are being asked to "waive"—that is, give up—a right. This will come up in two ways: (1) the agreement may state that you had an opportunity to consult your own attorney and waived it, and (2) you are asked to give up your rights to support or alimony and property division under state law. Don't waive anything until you understand what you are giving up—and if you do, make sure that's what you want to do.

Review the disclosures carefully. Make sure the sections where each party discloses their assets is complete and accurate as far as you can tell—and that your soon-to-be spouse has assigned a value to each of his assets. You should know what each of you are worth and what the prenup is asking each of you (or just you) to give up in the event of divorce or when one of you dies.

Ask lots of questions. Here are some of the questions you should be asking your attorney after the attorney has had a chance to review the prenup:

- What events does the prenup cover—divorce, separation, death of one spouse?
- What are my rights to property division and support under state law in the event of a divorce or if my spouse dies? Does the agreement ask me to give up these rights? If it does, does it give me less of a share of my soon-to-be husband's estate than that guaranteed by the law?
- Under this agreement, what happens to property acquired during the marriage? For example, suppose we buy a house together. Whose name will be on the deed? Both of ours or only his? Who gets it if we divorce?
- How will we divide earnings and income we both generate during the marriage? If my soon-to-be spouse has a business or a rental property that brings in money or that increases in value, will I get a share of those in the event of divorce or when he dies?
- I plan to step-down my career to take on more than half of the housekeeping or child-caring responsibilities. If I di-

vorce, does the prenup establish how I will be compensated for this work?

- There's a chance I'll receive an inheritance from someone during the marriage. What will happen to that money? Will it be my separate property, or will it be divided in the event of a divorce?
- Are you satisfied with my fiancé's disclosure of assets, or do you want more information? (If your attorney wants more information, allow time to get it.)

These are some things you can do if you are asked to sign a prenup. But perhaps the most important thing you can do is not to be afraid to ask for a fair deal—you deserve that.

CONCLUSION

Earlier in the chapter, I mentioned that one of the main reasons women sign prenups that they later regret is that they assume theirs will be a picture-perfect marriage: they believe their soon-to-be spouses will never do anything without their best interests at heart and their relationship won't end in divorce. But another reason is they worry that negotiating the agreement—asking for more—might signal that they don't trust their spouses or that they are greedy and want to take as much of their fiancé's hard-earned money as possible.

But getting a prenup that treats you fairly doesn't mean you don't trust your fiancé or that you are a gold digger. And it doesn't mean a divorce is inevitable. It just means you'll be protected in case something unexpected happens. It's just smart, like having life insurance. You should want this for yourself and your future. And your fiancé should want this for you too.

3

HOW DIVORCE LEAVES WOMEN OUT IN THE COLD

Divorce can be one of the most emotionally painful events in a person's life. Regardless of who filed for divorce, the raw feelings that follow the breakup of a relationship you've invested heavily in are compounded by fears of an uncertain future. When you are in the throes of divorce, it's easy to react emotionally, rather than strategically, about the legal and financial aspects of splitting up.

That's why it's crucial to understand how divorce laws routinely contribute to stripping women of wealth they helped create because not only is divorce an emotionally painful event but it can be a financially devastating one for women. Statistics, in fact, show that women's standard of living goes down after divorce, while men's goes up.[1] Divorced and separated women have the highest rates of poverty among older women,[2] but women of all ages typically slide down the standard-of-living scale after divorce. Why is that the case, and how can you protect yourself?

EQUAL IN THE EYES OF THE LAW
BUT UNEQUAL IN PRACTICE

It may seem hard to believe that in the past, in some ways, divorce laws protected women better than they do today. But ironically, it's true.

Before the 1960s, the law saw a man's duty to support his wife as a lifelong responsibility, one that could not be tossed aside by divorce or prenuptial agreements. To get a divorce, a spouse needed to show "fault"—meaning they had to show the other party had wronged them in some way. For example, a woman needed to show her husband had mistreated her or had had an affair or had abandoned her—and if that was the case, the husband would pay for these wrongdoings in the divorce settlement. Women were not expected to "bounce back" or "get back on their feet" after a divorce.

These old laws were certainly patronizing and demeaning to women. They assumed that women were incapable of earning a living and would always need a man to support them. And they were also unfair to men: the husband almost always had to pay alimony or spousal support—that is, he had to support his wife financially after divorce. No court even suggested that a divorced wife could get a job and earn her own living. Even if she was perfectly capable of doing so, the ex-husband was still expected to support her.

But the 1970s saw a revolution in divorce law. "No fault" divorce became available in many states, allowing spouses to file for divorce without showing that the other spouse had done anything wrong—but just because they wanted out of the marriage. At the same time, divorce laws started to catch up with the women's rights movement that was growing and seeking legal equality between the sexes. Courts no longer assumed that women were incapable of working and supporting themselves or that they needed lifetime protection. Since then, the law has seen marriage as a "partnership of equals," and financial support and the division of a married couple's property is decided based on need and fairness, not on stereotypes based on the spouse's gender.

This seems fair—and even desirable. Isn't that what women wanted all along? The trouble is that, in reality, women are still not equal to men. Women are still much more likely than men to be the financially dependent partner in opposite-sex marriages. Today, more than 40 percent of married women have left the labor force and earn no income, a significant number of them to take care of the home, children, and elderly relatives.[3] This statistic does not include those who have cut back on career or work to spend more time at home. Even wives who work outside the home earn less than half of what married men do.[4] Women with many children, and women with births spaced out over several years, earn least of all.[5] Whether employed outside the home or not, women still do more housework and childcare than men.[6]

These differences have huge implications for women's ability to accumulate wealth: higher-earning mothers' career cutbacks cost them an average of one million dollars per lifetime, while lower-earning mothers lose about six hundred thousand dollars. Leaving the workforce for only two or three years costs women an average of a 30 percent drop in lifetime earnings.[7]

Because of these differences, women are most often in a financially unequal position to their husbands during their marriage—it is rarely a "partnership of equals" as the law would have it. In fact, when women sacrifice professional opportunities because they have to take on a larger share of child-rearing and household duties, their husbands often benefit precisely because it gives them more freedom to devote time and energy to advance professionally and increase their earnings potential and wealth. Yet the law ignores this reality and treats men and women as equal in marriage and during divorce. By doing so, it siphons wealth away from women who, though financially dependent on their husbands, helped to create "his" wealth—and by the way, helped to create it with the implicit understanding that it would be shared in the marriage.

There are two main areas in which divorce law, by treating women and men equally, actually disadvantage women financially: when it determines alimony (also known as spousal support) and when it divides a couple's property. Let's take a look at these two areas.

WHY ALIMONY RARELY HELPS WOMEN IN DIVORCE

Alimony, or spousal support, is the financial support that a person may have to pay their financially dependent spouse for a period of time after a divorce. Alimony is meant to be a way to allow financially dependent spouses to maintain their standard of living until they "get back on their feet," for example, by getting the education and skills they need to support themselves. But financially dependent spouses aren't always entitled to alimony—it's not an automatic right. Instead, they have to ask for alimony in divorce proceedings, and the court decides whether they are entitled to it at all, and if so, how much and for how long.

Some states take a more extreme position. Texas, for example, bans permanent alimony altogether and made it nearly impossible to get even temporary alimony. Texas law allows for alimony under only two circumstances: First, the spouse from whom alimony is sought was convicted of a crime involving family violence within two years prior to the divorce action. The second circumstance requires that the marriage have lasted ten years and that the financially dependent spouse not have enough property—after the property division—to provide for her basic needs. In addition, she must show that she can't work because of a mental or physical disability, has to stay home and care for a child with a mental or physical disability, lacks the skills to get a job to support her basic needs, and so on. This isn't the end of the restrictions on alimony in Texas, however; there's a long list of additional ones. The point is that it's almost impossible to get alimony in Texas. This is an extreme example, but it's not an unusual attitude.

Now that women and men are seen as equally competent to earn a living, courts grant very few and very stingy alimony awards. Texas isn't the only one. A bill has been submitted to the Florida legislature that would ban lifetime alimony and makes it easier for ex-spouses to stop paying alimony when they retire (to date, the bill's fate has not been decided). On paper, when it comes to alimony, the law treats men and women equally: a wife with a full-time career is as likely to have to pay alimony as a husband with one. The trouble is that this equal law falls on unequal ground: 96 percent of those receiving alimony are women, not surprising given women are more likely to be the financially dependent spouse. That's why limited alimony awards have a disproportionate impact on women. They don't give women their share of wealth they helped create, and they don't give them the opportunity to start creating their own.

Even when a court does allow alimony, it always ends if the ex-spouse gets remarried. Given the disproportionate number of women receiving alimony, this is an example of latent sexism creeping into the law: the underlying assumption seems to be that any man a woman marries will support her financially. But what if a woman receiving alimony gets remarried to an older man who dies soon thereafter? Or to someone who does not earn enough to support the couple? These scenarios clearly do not apply in all—or even most—cases, but the law does not even consider the specifics of the particular situation.

Even when a court does grant alimony to help the financially dependent woman "get back on her feet" and return to full-time, self-supporting work, it rarely accomplishes its intended goal. Many divorced women are in their late forties and older, and age discrimination among employers makes it much harder for them to get well-paying jobs. That's one of the many reasons wealth increases much more slowly for postdivorce women than for post-divorce men, especially for the rising number of women over fifty getting so-called gray divorces. Sadly, a quarter of these women live in poverty.

In a nutshell, only between 10 and 17 percent of divorcing women get any spousal support.[8] Fewer than half of women married fifteen years or more get support.[9] Even mothers of minor children who have custody only get support 25 percent of the time.[10] And when they do, the support is small and brief. So when it comes to holding on to wealth created during the marriage, alimony rarely does the trick. The money is in the property. And yet, as with alimony, the laws about how property is divided after divorce typically disadvantage women.

Before we get to the property part, though, let's talk a bit more about spousal support. Earlier I mentioned in passing that alimony almost always ends when the spouse remarries—sometimes even when you move in with someone else. Eleven states make this automatic: you move in with someone, alimony ends.[11] This might seem fair at first glance, but if you look at it carefully, it isn't actually that fair to women. For one thing, the alimony is often cut off without any determination of the spouse's financial circumstances.

Consider, for example, the case of Helen and Anthony, who divorced after a twenty-six-year marriage.[12] During the marriage, Helen worked as a full-time homemaker and caretaker of the couple's children while Anthony pursued his career in banking. By the time they divorced, Anthony was earning $158,000 a year as a bank executive while Helen, having finished only two years of college and worked as a full-time homemaker, had no marketable skills. A court ordered Anthony to pay $500 per week in alimony and $300 per week in child support. Helen soon found work as a part-time medical assistant earning $90 per week. One and a half years later, Helen married again, and Anthony petitioned the court to terminate her alimony, which it did.

So far, you may be thinking this all seems fair. When Helen married again, she combined her income with her new husband's in a single household, significantly adding to her financial resources. Allowing her to keep collecting alimony seems to allow her to unfairly "double dip," doesn't it?

On the other hand, shouldn't we look at the specifics of Helen's situation? As it happens, Helen's new husband earned $28,000 a year and paid $7,800 of that in child support. His income was $184 a week; hers, as you recall, was $90. She had weekly expenses of $588. By contrast, Anthony's salary was now $180,000, and the value of his assets had also increased. The trial court said that Helen's financial circumstances had not improved enough to justify cutting off the alimony.

Anthony appealed, saying Helen hadn't shown that her current circumstances merited the continuation of alimony, even though she was barely meeting her needs and Anthony was earning even more than he had when they were married. The judge on appeal sent the case back for another trial, saying Helen had to prove that her remarriage had *not* changed her financial circumstances. Ever tried to prove a negative? It's not easy.

And you can probably imagine other scenarios that could make this "support-ends-with-remarriage" rule unfair. For example, given that divorce often occurs—as in Helen's case—later in life, what if the second spouse passes away shortly after the remarriage? That leaves the wife in a pretty bad place: her support is now cut off, and she doesn't have the support of the second spouse, whatever that was worth. Or what if the second marriage ends in divorce? And remember, some states end alimony even if the spouse just starts living with someone, regardless of how they arrange their finances.

So keep this in mind. Most support orders have this written into them, and many states just apply it even if it's not. If you are receiving spousal support, you may want to compare the financial benefits of cohabitation and remarriage before you take that step.

You may be thinking, OK, I can just make sure that the person I live with and I keep our finances separate; that way, I can prove that I'm not getting support from that person. This might seem to avoid the problem; after all, the point is to let your ex stop paying support if you're getting it somewhere else, right? Well, not exactly.

First, some states, as I've said, stop alimony payments automatically if you move in with someone, no questions about the financial details asked. For example, when Monica got divorced after more than twenty years of marriage and four kids, the court ordered her ex-husband James to pay her $1,400 a month in alimony.[13] Two years after the divorce, she started dating Donald, and three years later, James filed a petition to terminate support payments because he claimed Monica was living with another man—grounds for termination under Illinois law. James told the court that Donald often slept over at Monica's house, they took vacations together, and they spent holidays together. All this was true, but Monica argued that she was not receiving any financial support from Donald: each paid their own bills, Donald had never bought anything of value for Monica, and they didn't own any land or personal property together (in fact, Donald was retired). No one disputed Monica's claim that the two of them were financially independent. But it didn't matter whether Monica was now better off financially—the court said the mere fact that they lived together was enough to cut off her support payments from James.

This left Monica in exactly the same position she was in when the divorce court determined that she needed $1,400 in support—only now she no longer got the support. Her financial circumstances were unchanged; no one was disputing that. She lost the alimony simply because her boyfriend slept over at her house a few times a week. And some states calculate not what the partner is actually contributing to your shared finances but what they could or should be contributing.[14] Theoretically, alimony is awarded based on need, but these termination cases show that's not really true.

Even when courts do look at whether the new relationship is helping the ex-wife financially, it might surprise you to learn what they consider financial help. Turns out, it doesn't have to involve contributing money. Nancy got divorced in her fifties and didn't have a job,[15] so the court ordered her husband to pay her monthly alimony. A few years after the divorce, Nancy met Bob, and a year after that, he moved in with her. Bob contributed nothing to the household expenses, and he didn't pay rent. But he cleaned the pool, mowed the lawn, washed the car, and helped with a few other chores around the house. The court said these were valuable services and were worth money to the ex-wife—and that therefore her financial circumstances had improved enough to justify cutting off her support payments. It even compared Bob's lawn mowing to a housewife's unpaid labor in the home—you know, exactly the kind of labor courts tend to ignore when splitting up marital assets in a divorce. A bit ironic, isn't it?

Oh, and you might be surprised by how courts define "living together." In Beth's case, her ex-husband John asked a court to terminate alimony, claiming that she was living with her boyfriend, Al.[16] Al was in the construction business and was living at various sites of construction projects all over the country almost all the time: he testified that in the course of his relationship with Beth, he had lived in Colorado, Florida, and several different places in Alabama for several months at a time. Nonetheless, the court decided he was living with Beth. How did it get to this surprising conclusion, you ask? Well, Beth and her daughter had visited Al at one of his construction sites for three weeks, and Al had traveled to North Carolina to attend Beth's daughter's college graduation, and between jobs he stayed with Beth. So the court found that they were living together and terminated Beth's support.

Some couples go the bizarre lengths to avoid these consequences. After her divorce from John, Katherine started seeing Michael and formed a serious relationship.[17] Two years later, John petitioned a court to cut off her support because he said the two were living together. In fact, the two had gone to pretty extreme lengths to *avoid* living together: Michael had bought a house that had no heat, gas, or hot water, where he slept every night rather than sleeping at Katherine's. It didn't do any good; the court found they were living together anyway. And this was a state with a rule of automatic termination of alimony. Katherine tried to explain to the court that even if it found they were cohabiting, it shouldn't cut off her support because Michael wasn't helping her financially; in reality, he was worse off than she was, and she sometimes had to lend him money. Even if there was cohabitation, it hadn't lessened her need for alimony. But her actual need didn't matter: if the court found that they were living together—whatever that meant—it was terminated.

By the way, in case you're wondering, these cases are pretty unpleasant to read: they're full of testimony about whether people were having sex, and how often, and who bought groceries on this date and who stayed over at whose house on that one. All of this raises the question, what justifies this public prying into people's intimate lives? Is it that important for courts to be able to get ex-husbands out of paying support to ex-wives who haven't worked and are almost always financially worse off than they are—even if the new relationship clearly isn't improving her financial situation? Well, the answer seems to be yes. Maybe I digress a bit here, but it helps you see how things are often stacked against ex-wives on the alimony front.

So, the alimony is of limited help in setting you on the path to replacing your wealth. What about the property division then? The property is where the real money is anyway.

THE MONEY IS IN THE PROPERTY—AND MEN USUALLY GET IT

Over the course of a marriage, a couple is likely to share and accumulate a lot things—from a car to a house, savings accounts, and income to pay expenses for the family and to buy other things jointly. All of their financial assets—bank accounts, retirement accounts, and IRAs, for example—and nonfinancial assets—cars, real estate, valuable antiques, or collections (wine, books, you name it)—are considered "property." When a couple divorces, how that property is divided fairly is often one of the sources of most tension. And for good reason: the stakes are often high, and the rules for how property should be divided are complicated and vary significantly by state.

Forty-one states follow a system of what's call "equitable division of property" at divorce. Note that "equitable" means fair—not "equal." These states give judges a lot of leeway to divide property between the spouses in whatever way the judges think is fair, rather than just giving it to the person with title to the property or the person who literally bought it. Judges in equitable division states consider a lot of factors when dividing property, including the following:

- The amount of "separate property" belonging to each spouse. In equitable division states, "separate property" refers to property brought into the marriage by one of the spouses or property one of the spouses received as a gift or an inheritance during the marriage.
- How much a spouse's separate property has increased in value during the years of the marriage—and whether the other spouse contributed in some way to that increase.
- The amount of "marital property"—financial and nonfinancial assets—acquired jointly or with joint funds during the marriage.
- How long the couple was married.
- The spouses' ages and their ability to support themselves after the divorce.

Such a range of factors gives judges in these states enormous discretion over who gets what when the marriage ends.

In the remaining states (Arizona, California, Idaho, Louisiana, Nevada, New Mexico, Texas, Washington, and Wisconsin), the law follows a system called "community property." In these states, the law defines which property is considered part of the marital pot, what is known as "community property." Community property typically includes money that either spouse made during the marriage (including financial assets like stock, investments, and so on), any assets that were bought with that money, and any debts accumulated during the marriage. In community property state, "separate property" typically includes property a spouse brought into the marriage or inherited during the marriage.

The law in these states is that each spouse has a 50 percent share in the marital property. This seems as if it would work out more fairly to the financially dependent spouse, right? It's based on the notion that each spouse contributes equally to the acquisition of wealth within the marriage, whether through paid or unpaid labor. This means that the wife owns half and has equal management rights over the assets.

Fair enough—this does sound as if it would achieve more equitable results. The trouble is that this overall approach is full of loopholes, which I'll explain, and it doesn't affect how money is managed in the home. While equal management of community assets is the general rule, several states (California, Louisiana, Nevada, and Washington) recognize a "business" exception to the equal management rule. This means that a spouse who is a manager of a business has the right to make decisions regarding business assets without spousal involvement. If a spouse incorporates his business to form a corporation, partnership, or limited liability company, he essentially has control of all community assets titled in the name of that business, even if the law defines them as marital assets. For example, if company stock is registered in that spouse's name, only he can sell it—and he can sell it without the consent—or even knowledge—of the other spouse.

On an even more basic level, when a working spouse gets a paycheck, it is made out to him and deposited into his account. While many couples have joint accounts, there is no rule that they have to. This is true of all sorts of financial assets: checking and savings accounts, IRAs, and retirement accounts. The spouse whose name is on the account has exclusive rights to manage these accounts, even though they are community property. In fact, the law actually bars the spouse whose name is not on the retirement account from making management decisions about the account— decisions about investing, how much to put aside for retirement, and so forth. Decisions about retirement accounts affect women disproportionately since they tend to live longer and are more likely to need the support for longer in retirement. Yet if you are not the working spouse, or not the working spouse with the retirement plan, you have no say in how those savings are made or managed. Most importantly, community property laws do nothing to affect who manages money within the home.

Once a judge has determined what goes into the pot, in all but three community property states (California, Louisiana, and New Mexico), the law still only requires equitable, not equal, division of that community property. So while in theory community property laws seem to promise a fairer outcome, it's not always so. Equity and fairness are pretty subjective standards. As in equitable division states, judges in most community property states have a huge amount of discretion to tailor the division of community property to their own prejudices and beliefs.

For example, if, after years of being under- or unemployed for the sake of taking care of the house and children, a woman's career and wealth-earning prospects are less bright than her husband's, what looks "equitable" to many courts—say roughly half of the community property—might not really be fair. Also, a court may award property to one spouse that looks fair in terms of dollar amount but may still be unfair in terms of the assets distributed. Take the case of the family home. Because in most divorces involving children women get custody, courts also often give women the house, since it is assumed it is better for the children to stay in their home. Now it may look like the woman has received a really valuable asset—but it comes with costs. Often she has to pay the mortgage on the house on her own, and of course, she has to maintain it. Any real property like a house has limited cash value unless you sell it or take out a home equity loan, which can be expensive. You can't use a house itself to pay bills and buy groceries. The husband, on the other hand, may be awarded liquid assets—cash—such as pension plans and investment accounts, which are much more useful in day-to-day living and that can be invested—the opposite of the need to borrow against an asset like a home to make ends meet.

There are also many exceptions to the general rule that any-thing that enters the marriage becomes part of the marital pot to be divided. And these exceptions tend to favor the spouse with more resources or with a full-time job or business—typically men. For example, under Texas law, profits from a separately owned business earned during the marriage are community property. But if the owner simply incorporates the business—that is, he changes its corporate form by filing some paperwork—the profits can be held by the corporation as "retained earnings" (meaning they are now considered to be owned by the corporation, not the spouse) and magically transformed into separate property.

There's yet another way even community property laws, which are presumably fairer to financially dependent spouses, do not properly protect women—and that is through community proper-ty management rules. This is how they work: Before the 1970s, in community property states, the husband had controlled the com-munity property, that is, even if the property was shared, he could do whatever he pleased with it. For example, if the husband wanted to sell their house and the wife didn't, he could do it (although the wife did have veto power over the husband selling anything that she had brought into the marriage). The only point at which wives could really benefit from community property was at divorce or death, when they were entitled to half of it. This all gradually changed in the first half of the twentieth century. Just as the court started to see marriage as a partnership of equals, com-munity property states began to accept a gender-neutral approach to community property management.

Technically, today, every community property state except Tex-as has an "equal management of community property rule"—that means both spouses have equal control over the management of the community assets. For example, this means both of them must agree to sell real estate that the couple acquired during the mar-riage. Unfortunately, this rule masks inequality rather than elimi-nating it—and so, once again, perpetuates it. There are two prob-lems with this rule: First, it presumes both men and women have equal control over their assets within the home, which study after study has shown not to be the case in the majority of heterosexual marriages.[18] In most marriages, the husband controls the finances. Second, there are many exceptions or ways to circumvent this rule that statistically advantages men.

Financial assets—bank accounts, retirement accounts, and IRAs, for example—are exempt from community property management. If stocks are registered in one spouse's name, they may be community property, but only that spouse can sell them. When a spouse receives a paycheck in his name and deposits it into his separate account, it may technically be community property but the other spouse can't access the money. A couple's nonfinancial assets—such as a car, a house, real estate, and business equity—are not even subject to equal management at all. Rather, they are controlled by the person whose name is on the title. In four states (California, Louisiana, Nevada, and Washington), a so-called business exception to the equal management of rule means only the legal manager of a community property business can make decisions about that business.

In reality, "equal management" applies to a very small percentage of a couple's assets in community property states. So much of what is considered community property actually falls under one spouse's exclusive control. And the spouse most likely to be in charge of these assets is the one working full time or running a business full time. Guess who that is statistically likely to be? The husband. This rule disproportionately gives men a chance to deplete the community estate in anticipation of divorce, leaving little wealth to be shared with their wives. The only recourse for divorcing women is to spend large sums on forensic accountants to uncover the trail of transactions that depleted their community property.

For all these reasons, a financially dependent wife in a community property state is often no better off than one in a separate property state during divorce. Both systems are more likely to give men a chance hold on to more of the wealth that was created during the marriage and to control the couple's assets, allowing them to hide them. For example, it is perfectly legal for a spouse in a family business to agree to defer his salary so it will be paid to him in the future, making his income look a lot smaller than it actually is when it comes time to divide the couple's property and determining spousal support. There is nothing illegal about this, and no reasons wives can't do the same thing. It's just that, as in all the other instances mentioned in this section, it plays out unfairly when you consider the financially unequal positions that men and women often still have today.

When it comes to division of property, perhaps the most egregious way in which the law cheats women out of wealth they actively helped create is by refusing to recognize two incredibly valuable assets as property: a degree and a business's "goodwill."

THE DIPLOMA DILEMMA

During a divorce, distributed property or wealth represents women's, or any stay-at-home spouse's, share of the family unit to which they contributed—a return on their investment in the joint enterprise of marriage. It also often determines what trajectory a former wife's life will take. But all equitable division and community property states (except one) refuse to treat a spouse's advanced degree, such as a medical license, as property. Even though it is often one of the most valuable assets in the marriage— and in a marriage between young people, often the only asset— courts generally refuse to award the spouse who helped the other earn that degree a share of that spouse's future earnings. This is the case even when that spouse worked to support the degree earner through school, paid all the bills, took on all the work of running the household and childcare, gave emotional support, and gave up career opportunities of her own, all because she—and all too often it is she—assumed the two of them were building a life and future together through mutual effort and sacrifice.

Take, for example, Aisha and Jamal's story. The couple married just after college, before Jamal started medical school. Although Aisha had planned to go to law school, they decided that she would put it off until he finished medical school and started his practice. They also decided that she would support them both by working as a receptionist and taking care of the home so Jamal could focus on studying. After medical school, Jamal was accepted into a prestigious ophthalmology internship program, but since it didn't pay well Aisha stayed with her receptionist job. At the time she believed her sacrifice was worth it: once he completed his training, she thought, Jamal could be making $500,000 within a few years and Aisha could go to law school full time and finally focus on her career and financial success. But toward the end of his internship, Jamal told Aisha he'd fallen in love with another intern in his program. He moved out and filed for divorce.

During the divorce proceedings, Aisha asked the court for a share of Jamal's future earnings, arguing that she contributed to the degree by supporting him and keeping house so he could succeed as much as he had. But the court rejected her claim, saying that degrees are not property that can be divided upon divorce. It ordered Jamal to compensate Aisha only for the share of her income as a receptionist he benefited from: $40,000.

Refusing to treat advanced degrees as property that can be divided fairly in the form of a share of future earnings is probably the first and foremost way the law cheats women out of wealth at divorce. This refusal is unfair because, as we discussed earlier, courts are less and less likely to grant alimony awards—and when they do they are usually very small and short lasting. It is especially unfair when the divorce happens—as it often does—shortly after the spouse has earned the degree: at this point, most couples don't have much property that can be divided. The degree is often the only thing of real financial value in the partnership.

So a spouse's only chance of getting compensated for her career sacrifices and all that she did so her partner could create "human capital" in the form of a degree or accumulated experience and skills that led him to advance his career is to get a share of his earning potential. Not giving the spouse a share of the benefits of that degree leaves her with little return on the investment she made thinking the degree was a joint marital effort to improve both their lives.

Even in cases where the spouses made an explicit contract to exchange financial support for the freedom to pursue and earn a degree—with the understanding that there would be a payoff for the supporting spouse in the future—courts have refused to honor it. That was the case with Cynthia and Thomas, who were married for twelve years and had one child.[19] When they got married, the couple agreed that Cynthia would give up her career as a veterinarian to work as a teacher, which would allow her to both support them financially and have time to take much of the housekeeping and child-rearing responsibilities while Thomas got his undergraduate degree. The understanding was that Thomas would then support the family after he graduated and Cynthia would devote herself to being a stay-at-home mother. Cynthia worked as a teacher for four years until Thomas graduated, but then he asked her to continue working to support the family so he could get a master's degree and law degree. Cynthia, who was now forty years old, reluctantly agreed, and also agreed not to have any more children. Even with his law degree, Tom was at first unable to earn enough to fully support the family, but he finally got a position at a law firm that paid him enough to do so—for the first time in eleven years of marriage. Three months later, Tom told Cynthia he no longer loved her and that there was no hope for the marriage.

During their divorce proceedings, Cynthia wanted to sue Thomas for breach of contract, and failing that, unjust enrichment, which means that a party who benefited unfairly at the expense of another should pay compensation even without a valid contract. She argued that the services she provided him—supporting him, keeping house, and raising their child—were of great value to him because they allowed him to get his degrees and the enhanced earning potential that comes with them. But the court dismissed both claims; it argued there could be no valid contract for one spouse to support the other because mutual support was the personal duty of spouses and could not be modified by a contract. For the same reason, it dismissed Cynthia's unjust enrichment claim, saying that such a claim could not be brought when the services provided were a duty imposed by law.

A few states do try to compensate the spouse who supported the other while he earned his advanced degree, but even these states fall short of fair treatment. For example, Oregon's law allows for the spouse to receive compensation for contributions that a court decides are "material," "substantial," and of "prolonged duration" to the other's "education and training." Usually, these terms mean that the spouse must have earned money to provide most of the support for the couple during the husband's schooling. Contributions such as housekeeping, childcare, and emotional support are less likely to be "material, substantial." Nor do these standards even allow for consideration of a spouse's career sacrifices. Courts tend to think in monetary terms and often define "material" that way; if a spouse helped pay for the husband's tuition or earned money to support the family while he was in school, that may be "material." Just staying home and taking care of the house and kids while he built his career is usually not.

Louisiana denies a spouse reimbursement for contributions she made to her spouse's ability to earn a degree if she benefited from the increased earning power during the marriage. It's hard to see how a spouse could fail to "benefit" from the other spouse's increased earning power. In fact, this law basically guarantees that the dependent spouse will not be able to maintain the same standard of living after the divorce, since the very fact that the couple enjoyed a higher standard of living proves that she benefited from the degree.

New York is the most progressive state in the country when it comes to treating advanced degrees as property, yet it still fails to achieve real equity. It does not award an automatic 50 percent of the spouse's future earnings. Instead, the court asks how much will the spouse who earned the degree make over and above what he would have earned without the degree, and how much the dependent spouse actually contributed to the spouse's ability to earn that degree and that enhanced income. Once the court has determined this amount—the marital part of the degree—it distributes it fifty-fifty and awards the dependent spouse a payment or payments representing the "present value" of that 50-percent share—in other words, the amount of money you would have to invest today to accumulate the full amount in the future. The smaller lump sum the spouse receives does not, of course, amount to the income she would have shared with her husband had they stayed married.

Refer to the case study at the beginning of the introduction (p. ix) for an example of this kind of unequal split of future earnings.

The arguments against considering an advanced degree "property" and awarding a spouse a share of future earnings vary. Some call the practice "involuntary servitude" because it locks the spouse who earned the degree into his career for a specific amount of time. He can't, for example, switch to a more satisfying career that pays less money because he might not be able to pay his former spouse if he does. Another reason many courts resist the practice is that they claim the value of the degree is too speculative, since a person's earning potential is based on how much and how hard he works—factors he alone controls. Another argument is that a degree is a personal achievement, attained by the individual effort and talent of the person who earned it.

But these arguments against treating degrees as marital property that can be "divided" at divorce don't hold water. First, it's deeply offensive to compare buying and selling human beings to asking a spouse who benefited from the contributions and sacrifices of the other spouse to compensate her when the partnership she was investing in falls through. Second, it is not difficult to calculate what various professions and specialties pay on average; actuaries do it all the time in wrongful death cases. And courts don't need to grant a spouse awards based on the maximum earning potentially. Finally, the argument that a degree is the individual achievement of the earner ignores all the forms of support—financial, emotional, and otherwise—that made it possible for a person get the degree.

The only fair solution to this "diploma dilemma" is to award the spouse who contributed to the other's ability to earn an advanced degree a share of the income the degree will produce.

PARTNERSHIP OR NOT?

Lorna and Gary were high school sweethearts who married in 1965.[20] When they got married, Lorna was a high school music teacher, but she left that job to become a full-time homemaker and mother. Gary got an MBA and was spectacularly successful, ultimately becoming the chairman, president, and chief executive officer of GE Capital Services, Inc., the financial services arm of GE, the largest department of one the biggest corporations in the world. For thirty years, as Lorna described it, she was a "perfect corporate wife." Throughout the thirty years she supported and enabled Gary's rise at GE. She not only ran the home and raised the children but also entertained GE executives with large dinner parties at the couple's home and traveled to social events and business trips with her husband. She described her job as that of "mother, housemaid, cook, childcare provider, corporate wife and homemaker" and said it took twenty-four hours a day. She made her husband's success her sole focus and gave up teaching private piano lessons so she would be available for entertaining and traveling with him. GE sees itself as a "family organization" that treats employees and their spouses as part of the team. Lorna pretty much worked for GE; GE expected her to.

Lorna was such a devoted corporate wife that she threw a Christmas party for GE executives even as the divorce proceedings were starting, telling a friend privately of her distress and saying, "I do not know how I can go through with this party because of my marital problems"—but she did go through with it, and everyone who was there reported that it was a huge success.

When Gary decided he wanted a divorce, the estate's value came to $100 million. Lorna demanded half. Gary offered $8 million and $250,000 per year alimony. She refused. As she told the court, "Marriage is a partnership, and I should be entitled to 50%. I gave thirty-one years of my life. I loved the defendant. I worked hard and I was very loyal." A Connecticut court awarded her $20 million, one of the largest divorce awards in history.[21] But that wasn't what Lorna wanted—or what she deserved.

You might be having a hard time feeling sorry for someone who walked away with $20 million. She got enough to live well, that's for sure. But Lorna's didn't want enough to live well on. She wanted what she had earned. To understand Lorna's position, let's look at the role of the corporate wife.

To paraphrase Jane Austen, it is well known that a man seeking a senior executive position at a Fortune 500 must be in search of a wife. Being a corporate wife is actually a full-time job. These companies won't come out and say it, but off the record many company officials admit that a successful career requires "a better half."[22] They may not interview the wife, but as one official admitted, the company would make sure to invite her to dinner before they made a final offer to the husband.[23] (Today, this role might also be played by same-sex partners, even housekeepers,[24] but in general women still fill this role.)

The services they perform are of value to both the executive and the company, and they are not optional: the corporate wife is her husband's personal assistant, advisor, social hostess, wife, homemaker, community representative, cheerleader, and intelligence gatherer, to name a few. One such wife recalls entertaining business associates or clients every other weekend on average, and in doing so, smoothing the way for the deals her husband was trying to make.[25] Another one offered a less pleasant version when she said, "You are always on. It is a job more than any actual physical labor. I had to entertain people I couldn't stand. You have to smile when you don't feel like it [and] you had to perform well. If you didn't, when you'd leave a function, you'd hear about it."[26] Another recalls helping her husband, a partner at Arthur Young, the accounting firm, by taking business guests out to dinner when she was nine months' pregnant and wanted to stay home, and moving, against her wishes, from one coast to the other with three children under the age of three. She "just sat in my living room and cried." Then—like Lorna at the Christmas party—she got up and organized the move because employees who did not agree to move did not make partner.[27] Another wife rode to the airport with her husband when he traveled on business trips with three-by-five cards in her lap with the names of his clients and their wives and children, so he could make the client feel flattered that he remembered these personal facts.[28]

Even the IRS recognizes the business value of corporate wives. It allows couples to deduct a spouse's unreimbursed travel expenses when she accompanies him on business trips to assist him and entertain clients. So why don't courts get it?

This was Lorna's life. Does this make it easier to understand why she felt she had earned half the estate, and why she wasn't satisfied with $20 million? For all practical purposes, her life was as devoted to GE as Gary's was. You could even say more so—Gary could leave work, come home, and relax; Lorna's work for GE *was* the home. She was, as the other wife put it, "always on." Are you still surprised she wasn't satisfied with less than half the wealth? A lot less, actually—one fifth.

SHARING SOME GOODWILL

If your husband owns a business or professional practice such as a medical, dental, or legal practice, there is another intangible but very valuable asset that courts refuse to count as property in a divorce: the "goodwill" of that business or practice. Goodwill refers to intangible assets that contribute to the success of a business beyond the cash value of its assets (such as its income or physical equipment it owns). These intangible assets include the reputation of the business and its owner, location, effectiveness of its advertising, the skill of the people who work on that business, and so on.

Goodwill is often the most substantial value of a business or a professional practice, especially in small businesses or single-person offices such as a doctor or a lawyer might have. Statistically, more men than women are likely to own these businesses. But their financially dependent wives often contribute significantly to the goodwill of the business by helping their husbands run them either formally or informally. Still, courts routinely fail to divide the goodwill of a business fairly between spouses when they divorce and instead continue to cheat women of wealth they helped create.

Take, for example, the case of Daniel and Kleo, who were married for five years.[29] One year before they got married, Daniel set up his own chiropractic office and began practicing. During the marriage, he paid off his educational loans with marital funds, the couple both worked in the office, and for a time lived on the business premises. Daniel also traveled a lot on the weekends to workshops to further his professional skills, leaving Kleo to care for the home and their young daughter. Kleo even lent Daniel money both before and after the marriage to invest in the business. So that Daniel could reinvest his earnings in the business, Kleo worked two jobs in addition to her work in the chiropractic office.

Given her investment in her husband's practice, when the couple divorced, Kleo claimed she should receive a share of the goodwill of the practice. The court found that the practice had almost no goodwill value as of the date of the marriage, but by the time the couple broke up, the value of the business had increased to $134,463, of which $102,991 was goodwill. The trial judge found that the value of the practice was a result of the joint efforts of both parties and awarded Kleo 50 percent of the goodwill value of the business. Daniel appealed, and the higher court reversed, holding that the goodwill of the business was not property that could be divided between the spouses.

Courts that do divide the goodwill of a business or practice between spouses often differentiate between "business" goodwill, which comprises the overall reputation and other intangible assets of the business itself such as its location, and "personal" or "professional" goodwill, which grows over the years as a professional gradually gains expertise and experience in the field. Personal goodwill is, really, another form of enhanced earning capacity. The current trend is for courts to refuse to treat personal goodwill as property that can be divided.

But this distinction between business and personal goodwill makes little sense and ends up disadvantaging women who have contributed to their husband's business or practice. Personal goodwill, after all, is made up of the attributes a business owner or practitioner brings to their business or office: a reputation for punctuality, willingness to take time with clients, knowledge of the practice area, and so forth. These attributes, though personal, are not acquired in a vacuum. It's often the work of the financially dependent spouse that makes it possible for the professional—all too often the men—to attain and exhibit these qualities. By doing childcare and housework, and often working for free behind the scenes at the business or practice as Kleo did, wives allow their husbands to be punctual, take the time with clients, and gain experience, knowledge, and skill that increase the personal goodwill of the business.

THE TRUST TRAP

As I discuss in the chapter on spousal inheritance, trusts are a way of holding property so that one person, a trustee, manages it for someone else, the beneficiary. Suppose your spouse is the beneficiary of a trust. This probably means that the trustee sends a monthly or bimonthly (at some regular interval) check representing the income from the trust. Maybe this is what you live on, if it is enough; if not, maybe it's how you pay for your vacations, or medical bills, or private school tuition for the kids. Whatever the case, your probably won't get to share it when you divorce.

Here's another part of the trust trap: some states allow wealthy people to set up a special kind of trust called "asset protection trusts," which are specifically designed to shield the assets in them from spousal support, and often child support, claims. Of course, it's also possible to set up offshore trusts that are even harder to

access because it's not clear whether U.S. courts even have juris-
diction over them. I discuss trusts in more detail in the chapter on
inheritance.

GENDER BIAS OF COURTS AND ATTORNEYS

As we've seen, by treating men and women equally while ignoring
the reality of their inequality in most opposite-sex marriages, divorce laws cheat women out of wealth they deserve. A gender bias
among attorneys and judges only exacerbates this problem.

Women are overwhelmingly the financially dependent spouses
and don't have access to the same financial resources as their
husbands to pay lawyers' fees—and lawyers know it. Many refuse
to represent women in divorce cases because they know there is a
good chance they will not be paid, and judges are often reluctant
to order the husband to pay the wife's legal fees. If the wife can
afford a lawyer, she often hires a less skilled and experienced one
than her husband can afford and pays the price. In these situations, the husband's attorney can "starve her out," as the saying
goes, with frivolous motions and other delaying tactics.

Wives are also pressured to accept unfair settlements by threats
of custody disputes, a tactic lawyers representing husbands often
consciously employ: afraid of losing their children, women agree
to settle for disadvantageous terms. The trend of equal rights for
fathers has made these threats more credible—another unfore-
seen consequence of gender-neutral laws. The majority of judges
are still men, and, sadly, they often fail to understand, for example,
ways a wife might feel coerced by the threat of losing custody.

Judges often ignore the real unequal financial and power dynamics in a marriage that tend to put women in a disadvantage,
and in the process ignore even the most obvious examples of in-
competent and unethical representation. That's what happened to
Janice.[30] After several months of threatening divorce, Janice's husband, Lawrence, told her he had an appointment with a lawyer
and took her with him. Lawrence and his lawyer persuaded her to

sign a letter to another lawyer—who Janice did not know—asking him to represent her, and then they verbally discussed and agreed on the divorce. Janice never met this attorney, but he appeared at the final hearing saying he was representing her. He testified that he did not know whether Janice knew what property the couple owned and that the only information he had about an alleged oral agreement Janice made about property division was from the husband. Lawrence paid the attorney's fees.

Despite this blatant lack of even an attempt at competent representation, the judge signed the divorce decree based on the terms presented by Lawrence and the two attorneys. In fact, Janice did not even know about the final hearing and only found out about the divorce decree a month later when she consulted a new lawyer. "I didn't know what choices I had," she said. "My ex scared me, and I felt I had nowhere to go. He was mentally abusive and sexually aggressive, and he threatened to drag it out in court until I lost the little savings I had left. So I cut my losses and ran."

Janice's story is only one of many where women's unequal situation at divorce undermines their ability to negotiate aggressively. Their financial inequality leads to a lack of competent representation—and gender bias on the bench further ensures that such injustices are never addressed. The result is that women are cheated out of wealth that they helped create and of opportunities to accumulate assets and grow their own wealth for the rest of their lives.

COMPARE BUSINESS PARTNERSHIP LAW

I said in the chapter on cohabitation that it would be interesting to compare the property division on breakups and divorces with how the law handles the same issue in business partnership breakups. The answer is—not much better. Are you surprised? Often, the partner with less wealth who put in the "sweat equity"—did the work while the other person supplied the money—ends up with nothing, while the wealthy partner gets his investment back. I could go on and on about how unfair this is, but here's the thing: it often doesn't turn out that way because the partners avoid it by contract.

The partner with fewer assets who plans to be the one doing the actual work, rather than the investor, will probably insist on a contract to be paid a salary for her labor, either as she performs it or in the event the partnership ends. Either way, the partners would agree on the fair market value of the labor being done, and agree that this would be paid as an ongoing salary or in the event of breakup. If it is to be paid in case of breakup, the amount would be capitalized—that is, she would get the amount that she would have if she had been paid a salary and invested some of it and earned interest.

So business law actually does help you get a fairer deal: I'll show you how to protect yourself.

PROTECT YOURSELF!

Although divorce laws fail to acknowledge the all-too-common inequality between men and women in marriage, there are a few things you can do to get a better outcome if your marriage breaks up.

Protect Yourself Before Divorce Is Even a Question

When you marry you don't want to even think that your marriage might not last. But your emotional investment and belief in your partner might lead you to overlook the fact that your relationship, no matter how strong at the time, may not be a fifty-fifty partnership on paper. Here are some ways you can protect your wealth—which is smart even if you never divorce:

Understand and keep track of your property. Make sure you know what your husband and you own—what's your separate property and property you own jointly. If you bring property into the marriage, keep it that way. For example, if you own a condo before you got married and now rent it out, deposit the rental income in a separate, not a joint, bank account. Make sure you are listed in the title of any major asset you agree to own jointly, such as a home or a car.

Consider a prenuptial or a postnuptial agreement—one that protects *you*. If you agree to stay home or support your husband either financially or by taking a larger load of the housekeeping and child-rearing so he can earn an advanced degree, consider signing a prenup or postnuptial (similar to a prenup but signed after marriage) that guarantees you a share of the wealth you will help create with your sacrifices.

Seek Good Advice and Representation

If you are facing divorce, the most important thing you can do is ensure you are getting sound advice and representation. Here's how:

Get a lawyer. If you have to, beg or borrow to pay the fee. Legal representation always results in fairer property distribution for women who are financially dependent or vulnerable. Your attorney brings knowledge of the law, legal procedures, judge's preferences and temperaments, and experience with financial matters, such as options for dividing up pension plans. Property division can vary a lot even from court to court as individual judges have so much discretion. You need a lawyer who knows the different judges, their quirks and prejudices, and how to tailor your case to be most effective with them.

Pick a lawyer who will zealously represent you. The first ethics rule lawyers learn in law school is that they must "zealously" represent their clients' interests. But as I've shown in this chapter, some of them fail to do that when they represent women in divorce. You need an attorney who will represent you aggressively, especially if you are used to accommodating your spouse's wishes. A good lawyer will put herself between you and your husband and insist on getting a good deal. How do you find one who will do that?

- As I've mentioned, there is an elite group of lawyers in each state called the American Academy of Matrimonial Lawyers. These lawyers are chosen by the members of the bar for their commitment to zealous and ethical representation. It is the best place to start looking for a divorce attorney.
- Get references. Ask friends and use Facebook and blogs to get the names of divorce lawyers other women have liked. There are several websites that can help you as well, such as Avvo.com and SuperLawyers.com.
- Meet the lawyer. Most lawyers will give you a free—or low-cost—interview to discuss your case, and whatever you tell them is confidential, whether you end up hiring them or not. Also, once they have spoken with you and received confidential information, they are not able to represent your spouse.
- Make sure the lawyer also has expertise in tax and accounting or works with someone who does.
- There is a breed of lawyers, usually in solo practices, who specialize in mass-production divorces. Avoid them. You'll be able to tell them from a good lawyer easily: they will know all about your situation before you even explain it, and they will try to rush you into settling.
- Ask yourself the following: Do I feel comfortable with this lawyer? Am I able to tell this lawyer when I disagree with a way she or he wants to proceed?
- Be prepared to pay a retainer. Most divorce lawyers require a payment up front to begin representing you and will bill you for the work they do beyond what the retainer covers. This is the normal business practice of reputable attorneys.

Consider mediation carefully. Mediation is a process where the spouses negotiate directly with each other with a neutral third party, the mediator, acting as a kind of referee. The mediator's role is to make sure each party has an equal opportunity to speak, to get each party to express their concerns and priorities, and to get an agreement about the issues. Many courts today tout the benefits of mediation in divorce, arguing that it can better address each party's concerns and that it is a less hostile setting for settling disputes than a courtroom. This may be true in some cases. But the problem with mediation is that it tends to replicate power disparities between the parties. If your husband has more resources than you, then he also has many advantages in the negotiating process at mediation. He can hire negotiation experts to advise him on how to get an agreement that maximizes his benefits and minimizes yours. With more resources, he can also credibly threaten to walk away from—or drag out—mediation if he doesn't get what he wants. If he has more education than you do, he can also have an advantage by holding superior knowledge of property and its tax consequences. Mediators often have very brief training and are not always experienced in detecting or righting power imbalances in relationships. More importantly, a mediator is not your advocate. The mediator is not on your side and does not fight for you. The mediator does not stand between you and your spouse. Litigation, and representation by an attorney, on the other hand, can empower women. So how do you figure out if mediation is right for you? Answer the following questions honestly:

- Did your husband exercise financial authority in your marriage?
- Do you worry more about others than yourself?
- Do you tend to defer to those you perceive as having higher status than you (men, professionals, and people with power and money)?
- Does your husband have higher self-esteem than you?
- Have you been experiencing depression because of the divorce?
- If you've ever negotiated a salary for yourself, did you feel afraid to ask for more out of fear that the answer would be no?
- Are you uncomfortable with conflict?

- Does your husband have a higher level of education than you do?
- Is your husband older than you?

If you answer "yes" to more than one or two of these questions, you should not be in mediation. Yes, a lawyer can review a mediated agreement, but this is not nearly as effective as full representation. Lawyers are professionally obligated to protect the client's interests in negotiation, and they insulate the spouse with fewer resources from the power imbalances that resource discrepancy creates.

Getting through the Divorce Process

The divorce process can be incredibly stressful and painful. It's critical that you not let your emotions cloud your judgment. Here are a few strategies to help you:

Listen to your lawyer. Once you and your lawyer have agreed on your goals, do what your lawyer tells you to do. You're paying your lawyer a lot for her or his representation, so it doesn't make sense to ignore the advice. For example, your lawyer knows better than you how to act in front of the judge. If the lawyer tells you to limit what you say when you are giving testimony, do it. She or he knows when enough is enough.

Look at the whole picture when it comes to property division. Always think about the future value of assets as well as their present value. For example, retirement plans grow over time. Don't be fooled by present value. Don't let an emotional attachment to the family home make you accept it instead of potentially more valuable liquid assets, such as half the retirement funds.

Resist being intimidated. Don't let yourself be manipulated by your spouse's threats to get custody of your children (if you have any), or threats that you will get nothing if you don't agree to his terms.

Seek counseling. A good counselor will help you deal with the psychological aspects of going through a divorce. It can also help you to understand—and thus escape—the power dynamics in your marriage, which will make you a better negotiator.

Postdivorce

Remember that whatever support you may be getting will likely end if you get married again or even move in with someone. So before you make a move like that, it's a good idea to do some clearheaded thinking about your finances. Will you and your new partner combine your finances? And if you do, will you be better off than you would be sticking with the alimony?

Or at least as well off?

As in all these matters—prenups, cohabitating, and so forth—it's best to get ahead of the game. I sincerely hope your marriage is long and happy. But it never hurts to have a backup plan.

4

THE ROLE OF THE LAW
IN PERPETUATING DOMESTIC ABUSE

In 2006, Melinda, a social worker, was fired after her ex-husband called her employer and a city agency that had a large contract with her employer and falsely accused her of using drugs. Although she offered to take—and then passed—a drug test, her employer fired her because the employer believed the accusations of drug use, though unfounded, could jeopardize the company's funding and because her ex-husband repeatedly called the workplace. In another example, in 2005, Sarah, who worked as a maid at a hotel, refused to take calls from her abusive ex-boyfriend; when he began calling the front desk of the hotel several dozen times an hour, the hotel fired her.

Harassment at work deprives abuse victims of income, which they desperately need to stay out of abusive relationships. But all too often their employers simply fire them for the acts of their abusers that disrupt the workplace. Some states offer protection against this type of firing, but many do not. Being able to build financial independence by earning money is crucial to these women's ability to escape their abusers, but the law often fails to help them do so.

Here's another way the law fails abuse victims by depriving them of assets. In the last four years of her nineteen-year marriage, Donna's husband had become physically abusive toward her children and her. Although she left him many times, she always returned to him. She just couldn't pay the family bills on her own and was afraid her children and she wouldn't have a place to live. After one such "reconciliation," Donna and her husband began arguing. As she was trying to leave the house, he knocked her to the floor and began choking her. In the struggle, Donna managed to reach a gun she kept to protect herself and pulled the trigger. She killed him.

Although Donna was tried for the murder of her husband, she was found not guilty by reason of self-defense. Nonetheless, when she tried to claim her husband's life insurance policy, the insurance company refused to pay, citing the "Slayer Rule," a legal doctrine that prohibits murderers from inheriting property from the person they killed. Donna appealed the company's decision on the grounds that the killing was in self-defense (which means it would be justified and not require punishment), and the court ordered the company to pay.

This case is from the 1980s and might seem outdated to you. But make no mistake: the law in this case—that prevents an abuse victim who kills in self-defense from inheriting or getting life insurance proceeds—is the law in every state today.

Donna was fortunate to have enough resources to fight the insurance company, but many survivors of domestic violence are not. That's because financial abuse is almost always part and parcel of the cycle of abuse, leaving even those who are able to escape it in financial shambles and unable to acquire wealth for themselves.

A lack of financial resources can play a critical role in the cycle of abuse. Women with few resources are often vulnerable to abuse in the first place. Then domestic abusers—it's estimated that 85 percent of abusers are men[1] —block them from earning or having access to money that would help them escape the abuse. Abusers often prevent their victims from getting education or job training that would allow them to find decent employment. If they have a job, abusers sabotage them by making them miss work, harassing them at their place of work, and forcing them to show up at work with visible injuries. Abusers also often force their victims to turn over their pay, coerce them into applying for credit or even apply for credit in their victims' names (ruining their credit scores), force them to sign deeds over, sell their property, or take out loans for the abuser. They even force their victims to sign false tax returns, leaving them liable for back due amounts and penalties.

Given that abusers *intentionally* prevent their victims from gaining or keeping the financial assets and resources that would allow them to leave the abusive relationship, you'd think that our legal system would step in to protect these vulnerable women and their wealth.

But often it does not.

Many states allow employers to fire workers whose abusive relationships affect their work and also deny unemployment insurance benefits to workers fired for a reason such as missing work—even if they've missed work due to their partner's violence. The law also often prevents spouses from suing each other for acts unmarried people could sue for, making it very hard for victims to get financial compensation that could restore their assets and independence. Adding insult to injury, if women fight back and kill their abusers in fear of their lives, the law often deprives them of any life insurance proceeds they might have received. No law, on the other hand, bars abusers from inheriting from their victims or receiving their life insurance proceeds, as long as the abuser did not cause her death.

Now, if you are in an abusive relationship, your physical safety and that of your children, if you have any, are likely your most urgent concerns. There is help out there, and I beg you to get it. Money is often a critical secondary concern for many women who are abused—it might be for you too. Not having money or access to money is often the reason so many women feel trapped. In this chapter, I focus on this financial, wealth-destroying aspect of domestic violence. By doing so, I don't mean to disregard the many forms of violence domestic violence entails. I simply want to shine a light on how our laws often ignore the particular plight of battered women and, in doing so, deprive them of the very resources they need to escape the abuse and regain their financial footing.

In particular, there are three ways in which the law fails women who are abused: by not protecting their employment, by enforcing unfair distribution of property during divorce, and by preventing women from suing for damages related to the abuse. By the end of the chapter, I hope abused women will have a better understanding of how they can protect their wealth and evade the law's pitfalls. If you are one of them, I urge you to keep reading.

ABUSED AND OUT OF A JOB

Numbers worth paying attention to:

- One out of every five employed adults is a victim of domestic violence;[2]
- Twenty-four to 50 percent of domestic violence victims lost a job because of domestic violence;[3]
- Fifty-five to 85 percent took time off from work because of issues related to abuse;[4]
- Domestic violence caused 56 percent of abuse victims to take time off work at least five times a month;[5]
- Twenty-eight percent of victims have to leave work early at least five times per month because of violence;[6]
- Domestic violence issues makes 54 percent of victim employees miss at least three days of work per month;[7]
- Ninety-six percent of employed victims report that domestic violence affected their ability to perform their jobs.[8]

Philloria was a medical secretary in a doctor's office, where she was a punctual, diligent worker.[9] One night, about a year after she started work, her estranged husband broke into her apartment, raped her at gunpoint, and beat her severely with a lead pipe. The next day at work, she told one of the doctors she worked for, who in turn reported the incident to the doctor who ran the office, Dr.

Bryant. Dr. Bryant then told Philloria she was fired—not because of her work, which was excellent, but specifically because she was a victim of domestic violence.

Philloria sued for wrongful discharge. And lost. The court held that it was not illegal—or against public policy—for her employer to fire her because she was a victim of domestic violence.

Kim and her husband worked for the same large computer company. Kim's husband abused her at home and at work. One afternoon, he chased Kim down a hallway at work and assaulted her. Kim fled to a supervisor and told her that she was attacked in the office. In the next few days, Kim obtained a restraining order against her husband that included the workplace and told her employer about it, believing the employer would enforce it in the workplace. At first, Kim was hopeful when the human resources director at her company met with her and then with her husband, assuring Kim that everything would be "taken care of"; however, no action was taken against her husband. A few weeks later, Kim's husband assaulted her again at work, and she called the police who arrested him. Two days later, again failing to take any disciplinary action against her husband, the company revictimized Kim by firing her for "crying in the lobby."[10]

Philloria's and Kim's dilemmas are not that unusual. Between thirty and forty thousand incidents of on-the-job violence every year arise from intimate partner violence. Firing the victim does little to help, and it plays directly into the hands of the abuser. And yet it is still the approach of many employers.

All too frequently, men who engage in domestic abuse don't limit the hurt and damage they inflict to physical violence. Their goal is to completely control their victims. An effective way to do so, besides using physical force and threat, is by denying them financial autonomy. A common strategy for abusers is to make their victims dependent on them for money simply by sabotaging their very means of earning it: their jobs. If you don't have a job and make money, it is that much harder for you to leave the relationship. And work is a place abusers know they can find their victim.

Abusers not only put their victims' employment at risk by preventing them from getting to work at all—denying them transportation, sabotaging childcare, or destroying work clothes—but also often harass their victims at their place of employment, causing disruptions at their work and embarrassment. This strategy works: victims of domestic violence in the United States lose about eight million days of paid work a year, the equivalent of thirty-three thousand full-time jobs.[11] It's estimated that between 24 and 52 percent of abused women have lost a job due, at least in part, to domestic violence.[12] Women who are in the process of escaping from a domestic violence situation also risk their jobs by missing work due to court appearances, meetings with the police, doctor's appointments, and so forth. If you are in a domestic violence situation or trying to get out of one, this may well be happening to you.

Unfortunately, the laws don't always protect women or help them minimize the financial damage that domestic violence inflicts on them. In some states employers may fire workers whose abusive relationships affect their work, for example, if an employee misses work due to injuries or if an abuser shows up at the workplace to harass the victim and disrupts her workplace. Women who lose their jobs for such reasons are much less likely to be able to leave the abusive relationship without an income.

There are some bright spots: The laws in some states—California, Colorado, Florida, Hawaii, Illinois, Kansas, Maine, New York, North Carolina, Oregon, and Washington—provide some protection for abuse victims, giving them the right to take time off from work to address domestic violence issues without losing their jobs. And several states grant victims time off from work to go to court, to get a restraining order, for example, and some require an employer to grant leave to employees who need to seek medical care, move to safe housing, or take part in safety planning.[13]

Some victims of domestic violence, like Philloria, are even fired simply because they experience abuse. Employers might blame them for being in an abusive situation or think the only way to prevent workplace drama or even workplace violence is to get rid of her. While some states like California, Illinois, New Jersey, New

York, Oklahoma, and Pennsylvania, as well as New York City and Westchester County (NY), have passed laws making it illegal to discriminate against domestic violence victims (including firing them because of their status as victims), most states don't do much to protect them.

What complicates matters for many abused women is that the law in some states denies unemployment insurance benefits to workers who are fired for some fault of their own, such as missing work. In this way, abuse victims are further penalized; by missing work because of their partners' violence, they lose not only their jobs but also their unemployment benefits. This law perpetuates the cycle of violence by depriving abused women of the resources they desperately need to escape their abuse. Fortunately, the majority of states today have laws allowing people who have to leave their jobs for domestic violence reasons to get unemployment benefits. But employers are often not aware of them and still deny benefits to abused women simply by the way they report their unemployment status. For example, an employer might say a woman was fired for absences without explaining that the absences were caused by domestic violence, causing the state to deny her unemployment insurance.

The bottom line: victims of domestic violence often struggle to keep their jobs because of the very abuse they endure. Earning an income might be the only way for them out of their abuse—or to regain their footing. And yet the laws don't do enough to help abused women hold on to their jobs and earn an income.

NO FINANCIAL RESTITUTION FROM DIVORCE

You might think if a victim of domestic violence manages to leave her marriage and divorce her abuser, our laws would help make up for the financial abuse she's likely endured during the division of property. But few courts see the law that way.

Beginning in the 1970s, states began to allow couples to get divorced without a finding of fault on either side—called "no-fault divorce." Today, a couple can get divorced by merely asserting "irreconcilable differences" in every state. In general, the adoption of no-fault divorce by all states has been seen as a positive development because it has allowed spouses who don't want to be together anymore to free themselves without having to pretend one of them is having an affair—without messy litigation and without public humiliation. It also made divorce easier in most situations, including when domestic violence is involved.

But with no-fault divorce, courts order spousal support and property division without regard to either party's fault. With fault taken out of the equation, in most states, spousal abuse—even financial abuse—isn't a factor when the courts decide how to divide property. Only a few states consider acts of spousal or child abuse when distributing marital or community property: some consider acts of abuse relevant per se, that is, in and of themselves; others only consider abuse if it was "so egregious as to shock the conscience of the court" (not just regular, run-of-the-mill abuse, which apparently isn't shocking). [14]

Some courts consider abuse relevant to property division if it involved the squandering of marital assets or affected the wife's ability to support herself in the future. For example, one court ruled that the wife's impaired health—a result of domestic violence—justified dividing the property in such a way as to favor the wife because so much of her income after the divorce would have to be spent on medical care. [15]

In general, however, don't expect courts to distribute property in your favor if you are a victim of domestic violence and financial abuse.

SUING THE ABUSER

If a stranger came up to you on the street and hit you in the face, he'd be arrested and you'd be able to sue him "for damages," a financial award paid to compensate you for some harm done to you. Suing the person who hit you in the face for damages would allow you to at least get some compensation for the physical and emotional pain that you've suffered by his action.

But believe it or not, if your intimate partner hits you repeatedly—or worse, for years—in many states, the law makes it difficult or impossible to sue him. In fact, in these states, the law prevents spouses from suing each other for acts unmarried people could sue for. Where does this law come from? It's an old medieval law (yes, you read correctly, medieval) that states a husband and wife are one person: since you can't sue yourself, you can't sue your husband (I'm not kidding). But the law preventing spouses from suing each other also came about because of the courts' reluctance to get involved in matters between spouses, a zone generally considered too private for legal intervention.

Fortunately, as awareness of domestic violence has grown over the last fifty years, some courts have been willing to entertain these so-called interspousal torts. (A tort is a "wrong" that causes harm to a person and for which that person can sue for damages.) For example, Sheila sued her husband William for infliction of emotional distress because he "intentionally and cruelly forced her to engage in deviate sexual acts."[16] The trial court awarded her more than $15,000; the appellate court affirmed. William appealed to the state supreme court, arguing that spouses could not sue each other, but the state supreme court disagreed. It recognized intentional torts between spouses and upheld the verdict. Some of the torts victims of domestic violence might sue for include

- assault and battery (hitting),
- false imprisonment (not letting you leave the house),
- stalking (recognized as a personal injury claim in some jurisdictions), and
- intentional infliction of emotional distress (that is, acting on purpose in a way that causes another person great emotional distress and psychological harm).

Some states also allow victims of domestic violence to bring claims against third parties who knew about the abuse, or saw it, but failed to intervene, such as doctors, therapists, clergy, and landlords. Some states have even developed specific personal injury causes of action for domestic abuse. Jean Marie's case is a good example. She successfully sued her partner, Wilson, for causing her to have battered women syndrome by regularly and consistently assaulting her, breaking her nose, hitting her with his fists on repeated occasions, and hitting her with heavy cookware.[17]

Unfortunately, interspousal tort claims are rarely made. Why? First, in the states that allow you to sue your spouse for personal injury, courts still try to undermine this kind of lawsuit by refusing to allow interspousal torts to influence property division. Some courts even impose higher standards for personal injury cases between spouses than between unrelated people.

Thankfully, some courts are beginning to recognize the need to compensate abuse victims for the harms they have suffered: a victim in Maine got a $25,000 settlement in addition to her share of the marital estate when she sued her husband. A Virginia woman whose husband had pistol-whipped her won a $50,000 jury award.[18]

The second reason victims of domestic abuse often don't sue and seek damages from their abusers is that most insurance policies don't cover it. If someone slips on your icy driveway, breaks a leg, and sues you, your homeowner's insurance will likely pay for your defense and cover any damages award. Not so for suits for the kind of intentional acts that constitute domestic violence (such as assault and battery). So, in the case of person who slipped on your icy driveway, it might be worth it for that person to sue you—even if you aren't very well off—because your insurance will pay. But your insurance is unlikely to pay for domestic violence tort, which means a lawyer might be unwilling to take your case and might even discourage you from trying to file one. Few victims have the money to pay for a lawyer's fee up front, and few lawyers are willing to take such cases on a contingency fee basis—a common way to pay lawyers for personal injury claims—because it's very hard to win these cases.

Finally, many domestic violence survivors don't realize they can bring a claim for their injuries—these kinds of lawsuits are not common knowledge. There are no prime-time shows about lawyers who help abuse victims bring lawsuits that might raise awareness.

Despite these obstacles, some victims of domestic abuse have won significant damages awards. Carol sued her ex-husband, a surgeon, for damages after years of domestic abuse during which he shot her in the face, causing her to lose her left eye and hearing in her left ear, and requiring thirteen surgeries to repair shattered bones.[19] She won $10.9 million. In another case, a jury awarded Darlina a multi-million-dollar verdict because her husband beat her so badly when she was pregnant that she went into premature labor.[20]

Getting out of domestic abuse situations is very expensive. If you are a survivor of domestic violence, you might have medical bills, bear the bulk of childcare expenses, and receive inadequate spousal and child support, which the abuser may fail to pay anyway. In addition, you might be trying to set up a household independently, maybe without adequate job skills or education. A damages award could make some of your financial losses up to you, allow you to create a life for yourself and your children, and avoid getting trapped in an abusive relationship again. There might also be therapeutic benefit to suing for damages: a lawsuit may provide closure, offer public recognition of the harm done to you, and may make you feel empowered after years of feeling powerless.

PROTECT YOURSELF

If you are in an abusive relationship, the first step to protect yourself and your financial resources is understanding whether you are also a victim of financial abuse. If your partner does any of the following, then he might be financially abusing you:

- titles all the property in his name;
- prevents you from getting to your job or school (for example, by refusing to drive you there or by getting you to call in sick by making threats);
- controls your money or money you earn;
- refuses to give you access to or information about credit cards or bank accounts;
- keeps you on an allowance, making you report every penny you spend;
- makes you beg for money; or
- fails to pay child support but buys expensive gifts for the kids to get their affection.

These actions might be robbing you of your assets and will make it even harder for you get out of the abusive situation—this is exactly what your abuser wants. He wants you to be dependent on him.

So what can you do to protect your financial resources while you are still in an abusive relationship or have just gotten out of one?

- Consider opening a post office box so your abuser doesn't know where you keep important documents and valuables.
- Keep an eye on your credit report, keep track of bank account statements and credit card charges, and understand what property is titled under your name and your spouse's. It's critical that you stay on top of the finances, particularly of anything listed under your name—but don't endanger yourself in the process. Check out the website Womenslaw.org, which offers helpful resources and information on financial abuse.
- If your abuser has ruined your credit (by taking out loans or credit cards in your name and never paying them, for example), start the process of repairing it. This is a long, difficult

process, and the sooner you get started, the better. For more information, check the web pages of the National Consumer Law Center and Credit.com for helpful advice on repairing credit.

- If your abuser is harassing you at work or negatively affecting your performance or ability to keep your job, investigate what protections your state offers you in terms of keeping your job or receiving unemployment benefits. Many states have nonprofits that employ "employment advocates" who can help you work with your supervisors to create a safe workplace for you.

- If your abuser's behavior or harassment has led you to be fired from your job and having your claim for unemployment denied, consider appealing the decision to have your benefits denied. A legal aid lawyer can help.

- If you are about to get divorced or in the process of getting divorced, keep in mind that as a victim of domestic abuse (particularly if there was financial abuse as well), you may be able to get more of the property. Make sure you bring this issue up with your lawyer.

- Find out whether you can sue your abuser for physical and psychological harm. This may be a source of wealth for you, and if it is, you deserve it. A lawyer can help you. If you can't pay for one, check with your local legal aid association—they might be able to provide assistance or point you in the right direction.

Above all, ask for help. It's out there. Besides organizations that are ready to help victims of domestic violence in various ways, there are many organizations that help women navigate our complex legal and financial systems.

CONCLUSION

If you are currently a victim of domestic violence, you might already know how dangerous it is to be deprived of access to money on a daily basis. And if you are in the process of escaping from a domestic violence situation, then you know the critical role financial assets play in how quickly you can regain your footing after leaving your abuser. Money is essential to establishing an independent home, seeking the help you need (medical or otherwise), and feeling empowered. While your financial well-being might be secondary to your children's and your physical safety, it is nonetheless a cruicial resource that you must guard carefully. Protect it—and it might just prove to be your ticket to safety and freedom in the future.

5

CAREGIVING'S COST TO WOMEN

Hildegard was married to Michael for almost nine years.[1] Three years after they wed, Michael was admitted to the hospital for heart problems. Over the next few years, he was hospitalized several times until five years later, in one of those hospital stays, he had a significant stroke.

Michael, who now needed round-the-clock nursing care, pleaded with Hildegard to care for him at home rather than at a rehabilitation center. She suggested they hire a professional caregiver instead, but Michael was adamant that he wanted her to care for him. In return, he promised to transfer most of his separate property to her in his will. She agreed to take care of him, sacrificing, as she put it, the ability to have "an independent life" until his death.

Hildegard held up her part of the agreement, but Michael did not: he left his separate property to his daughter from a prior marriage, leaving Hildegard only $100,000 and his share of the property they owned together. Hildegard sued the estate, asking the court to enforce the agreement she'd made with her husband. But the court denied her the compensation Michael had promised because as a family member she had a duty to take care of her husband without expecting any pay.

At the heart of the court's decision is a legal rule that often results in injustice for those who care for a sick family member: the "family member rule." It states that caring for a family member is a duty and therefore can't be the subject of a contract; that is, you can't contract to get paid for something you are required to do anyway. According to the law, Hildegard could not be compensated by her husband as he had promised her for taking care of him. Many courts today still apply this family member rule.

While it might *feel* right that we have a duty to care for our elderly parents or an ailing spouse, the idea that we shouldn't be able to get any financial compensation for our efforts was born a long time ago, when families operated very differently. The "family member rule" evolved at a time when two or even three generations lived together in one house or close by—and when women were much less likely to work outside the home.

Today, people often move across the country for career or other reasons and don't always live close to other family members, especially to retired ones who could do some of the caregiving for family needs. And women, of course, are a big part of the workforce: 74 percent of women ages twenty-five to fifty-four have a job or are looking for one.[2] The "family member rule" doesn't take into account the sacrifices that people today have to make to care for aging parents or sick family members, such as cutting back on career advancement or giving up on careers altogether (and the potential wealth that comes with both).

Why doesn't it? Because the bulk of caregiving is done by women. According to the Family Caregiver Alliance, women account for 66 percent of caregivers and, on average, provide twenty hours of care per week. Men who care for a family member typically spend 50 percent less time doing so than women.[3]

The "family member rule" is only one of the roadblocks the law places on women's abilities to claim some reimbursement for their caregiving services—and another way in which our legal system siphons wealth from them. In a previous chapter, I showed you how the financial and career sacrifices women make to provide the bulk of childcare in a marriage are not always taken into account by the law during the division of property in a divorce. In this chapter I show how women are similarly penalized for caring for aging or sick family members. I also explain how you can protect yourself and your wealth when providing such care and what you can do if you are discriminated against for being a caregiver.

But first, let's look at what's at stake: how does caregiving affect women financially?

THE COST OF CARING FOR OTHERS

Caring for elderly parents, grandparents, sick spouses, and other family members is a considerable burden, regardless of how much you love the person you are caring for. Not only can caregiving be emotionally draining and a source of substantial stress (which often affects *your* health), but it can also have devastating economic consequences.

If you stay employed while providing care for a family member (the Family Caregiver Alliance estimates that 20 percent of all female workers in the United States are also family caregivers[4]), your work will likely suffer. Perhaps you need to cut back on hours, skip overtime, take time off, decline additional responsibilities, or forego investing in your professional development. The Family Caregiver Alliance shows, for example, that 33 percent of female caregivers reduce their work hours and that "caregiving reduces paid work hours for middle aged women by about 41 percent."[5] It also reports that 29 percent of female caregivers forego promotions and professional development opportunities, while 22 percent go on leave.[6] Twenty percent of women who provide caregiving end up going from full- to part-time positions.[7]

As you work or focus on your career less, your ability to accumulate wealth is greatly affected. First, your income is reduced, which in turn lowers future social security payments and pensions and deprives you of money to invest over time. Second, by passing on career opportunities or professional development, you also pass on the opportunity to earn higher pay.

The professional setbacks caregiving entails can be hard to recover from. These responsibilities tend to hit us women in our forties, and studies have shown that the job market offers limited opportunities for women that age. In fact, 11 percent of female caregivers end up quitting their jobs due to caregiving, reducing their social security benefits by a lifetime average of $300,000[8] — and consequently their ability to live in retirement.

A study from MetLife and the National Alliance for Caregiving calculated women lose an average $324,044 in compensation due to caregiving.[9] What this means in terms of wealth is even more alarming: women's average loss of wealth has been estimated at $659,139 per person over a lifetime.[10] In fact, if you are a woman who cares for a family member, you are two and a half times more likely to live in poverty than a woman who does not.[11] Your retirement fund will suffer by approximately $40,000 more than it will for a male caregiver.[12] As for pensions, you are less likely to receive one. If you do, it will likely be half of what men receive.[13]

Although caregiving comes at a great financial cost, the law fails to acknowledge the sacrifices of these caregivers. If you take care of an ailing parent or spouse and that person dies without a will, a probate court will not take into account the financial losses you've absorbed to be that person's caregiver when dividing the property—unless you have a written contract with the person you cared for (and a court enforces it). So if you are taking care of a loved one or foresee that you will have to in the future, your best bet is to make an arrangement with that person up front: either by getting paid for your caregiving at the time you are providing it or by writing a contract that specifies what kind of compensation you will receive to make up for these sacrifices.

TALK WITH LOVED ONES ABOUT COMPENSATING YOUR CAREGIVING

It's hard to ask a loved one to pay for you to take care of them; it's hard for you even to think you *should* get compensation—you're doing it because you love the person and they need you. Of course you wouldn't let someone you love spend their remaining years in a nursing home. Of course you'd choose to take care of them at home if you could. It seems mercenary to talk about compensation at all, but especially to ask a relative to put their intentions in writing.

Most agreements between family members are, in fact, based on spoken words, not written contracts. When your sick aunt tells you again and again that she'll leave you her estate to show her gratitude for your care, you feel comfortable relying on her words—that's how things are done in families. Asking for a written contract can seem cold and callous.

But an agreement between your parents or any other family member and you, similarly, doesn't undermine the love and affection between you. It's actually an expression of love and support—and the desire to make sure that you can care for the person as you want to do without condemning yourself to poverty. This is probably something the person whom you are caring for would want too.

Sit down with the person you are caring for and have an honest conversation. Tell them how much you love them and want to take care of them when they most need you. Share how much you can't stand the thought of them being cared for by strangers. Explain how you would really like to be able to help them as much as they need but that it comes at a great financial sacrifice. Show them how your work hours and income have or will suffer and how that affects your ability to save for retirement, secure a future for your own family, and so on.

Ask them for an arrangement that would make it more feasible for you to care for them the way you both want. You might decide on some sort of immediate compensation for your caregiving, or to draft a written contract that specifies what your duties will be and what your loved one will give you in exchange, or to work with a lawyer to draw up an estate plan for your loved one that includes an agreement to leave you whatever assets you agree on as a way to make up for your losses in salary and advancement—and wealth creation.

Of course, these situations can be complicated. There may be more than one child involved if you have siblings, one or more of whom are in a better position to provide care than others. You should all have a discussion about who can provide the care and how much each person can provide. Or there may be a grandparent who needs care and who is losing or has lost their capacity to make decisions about it. This is another family discussion everyone should have. Is one of you a guardian or trustee who can make decisions for the person, or is one of you willing to be? Having siblings can make the burden lighter on everyone if they share caregiving, or it may be that you all agree that one person will be the primary caregiver. Either way, if you can all agree on how this will work and what compensation the caregiver or caregivers will receive from the estate, it will make everyone's life easier and less stressful.

Surprisingly, coming to an explicit agreement may well make everyone involved feel happier and more secure with the arrangement. As time goes on, the person you are caring for will feel more confident in your ongoing services and maybe less guilty about all you're doing for them. And it might make you feel better and less anxious and resentful about the situation if you know that there is some security in it for you.

GETTING PAID FOR CARING

Contracts don't have to be a bad thing between family members. In fact, over the last fifty years or so, families have more and more been based on providing contract options to their members. Marriage itself is a contract. In two major religions—Islam and Judaism—the marriage agreement is literally a written contract (*nikah* in Arabic and *ketubah* in Hebrew) that sets out the rights and responsibilities of the parties toward each other, financial and otherwise. A *nikah* can be as specific as spelling out where the couple will live. These contracts do not seem to undermine marriage; rather, they strengthen it by emphasizing the mutual obligations and reciprocity inherent in it.

You might discuss with the family member you are caring for and everyone else involved about getting paid for your services. If this is an option—that is, if they have the funds to pay you an hourly rate or some other wage—note that doing so might affect their ability to be eligible for Medicaid in the future. You should consult an attorney who specializes in government benefits to find out about this: although Medicare and Medicaid are federally funded, the states each administer them according to their own rules, which can vary. Medicaid officials are often suspicious of agreements to pay a relative for care that they see as a way for the older person to deplete their assets in order to become eligible for state-funded services. Should the person you are caring for need to apply for Medicaid, officials will examine your agreement closely. They'll assess whether you were paid fair market value for your services, ask the person you cared for whether they intended to pay for the service, and determine whether the agreement was enforceable. If you are paid for caregiving services, you'll also need to consult with a tax attorney on how the income paid by your relative would need to be reported.

If your loved one already receives Medicaid, which covers some low-income individuals and those with disabilities, you might be able to receive compensation for your in-home caregiving through that program. (Medicare does not pay for in-home care.) In some states, the Medicaid rules sometimes allow that person to hire a family member to provide in-home care.

The problem, however, is that the hourly rates these programs pay are usually significantly lower than the state's average hourly rate for in-home care. Whatever pay you receive through Medicaid is unlikely to make up for your lost wages, and of course, they wouldn't make up at all for all the other financial losses you are likely to absorb, such as lost or reduced pension and social security benefits.

In general, getting paid for services you provide—especially if it's through a government program—can be tricky. But more important, it might not even pay the going rate for such services or adequately make up for your lost wages or professional losses. Your best bet is to talk with the person you are caring for and other family members about how they might be able to add more security to the financial future you are putting at risk for them by agreeing in writing to include you in their will in a meaningful way.

PUTTING IT IN WRITING

Another way a loved one can compensate you for caring for them is by promising to leave you some or all their assets after they die. If you are very close to the person you are caring for—a parent or spouse—you might have enough assurances that you are indeed in that person's will or trust. You might have seen a copy of the document or even have sat down with that family member and their attorney to put the will together.

Unfortunately, most of the time, you are not in a position to confirm that you have been included in the will or that the person has made provisions for you to receive what you've agreed to in exchange for caring for them. Even if your loved one promised to include you in his or her will, the person might forget, put it off until it's too late, or, worse, have a change of heart after you've spent years as a caretaker or be influenced by others to leave you out of the will. That's why it's important that you put in writing that the person you are caring for will make a will leaving you whatever it is you've both agreed to, or compensate you in some other way you both agree on.

As I discussed earlier, asking a family member to compensate you for taking care of them is emotionally challenging—asking them to put it in a legal contract even more so. But having your agreement in writing and signed by both parties is extremely important as it can prevent 90 percent of disputes that arise from them. You will have proof of the agreement when the person is gone and your loved one can be assured that their wishes will be carried through, and they will probably be able to stay at home longer, which the person probably wants.

A bit later, I discuss possible legal avenues to take if you do not have a written agreement or if the person you are caring for fails to fulfill his or her part of the deal. First, though, let's look at the contract.

Your agreement is a contract like any other contract—it will be governed by contract law, not wills law. It should state *why* you are entering into the agreement and what is being *"exchanged."* For example, it might read generally like this:

> Whereas [care recipient] suffers from X and is in need of intensive care. Whereas [caregiver] anticipates reducing her hours at work to provide the care [care recipient] needs and will suffer loss of income and opportunities at work and corresponding loss of social security, retirement income, and investment opportunities. Therefore, in consideration of caregiving services provided to [care recipient] by [caregiver] from [date], such services to include [for example, feeding, bathing, giving prescribed medications, transporting to doctor and hospital appointments], [care recipient] promises to leave [caregiver] the following assets out of [care recipient's] estate: [for example, $100,000, my house, my car, etc.].

Another way to approach this is to hire someone called a "licensed geriatric care manager" to visit the person at home and do an assessment of their health and caregiving needs. You will have to pay a fee associated for such an assessment that varies by state and region. You can also hire a geriatric care manager on a monthly or as-needed basis to do periodic in-home assessments as the person's needs change over time.

However you assess the person's needs, the contract should be executed *before* the date that care services begin and give a date for the beginning of the services. It should also explain the circumstances under which the parties can terminate the contract if they wish. And it should be signed by both parties. If you have an attorney, it would be best if she or he drafts this contract for you, but it's important for you to understand the requirements for a valid contract anyway.

One last piece of advice: keep track of the hours you spend caregiving and any expenses you incur. It's not a bad idea to keep a daily log of services you perform as proof that you fulfilled your part of the contract. It's also helpful to keep track of lost work opportunities as they occur—maybe you had to turn down overtime or a training seminar that could have led to higher pay. Write it down. This information could become important if the person you are caring for breaks their promise.

This is also the time to get powers of attorney, possible guardianship, wills, trusts, and health care directives signed, as long as the person has the mental capacity to do so.

WHEN PROMISES ARE BROKEN

As I mentioned earlier, even if the person you are caring for assures you that they will make a will leaving you what you've agreed to—and even if they sign a contract stating as much—they might fail to do it. Sometimes, people break their promises, as Michael did. The person you are caring for might forget to update their will or change their minds and leave their assets to someone else instead. What happens then?

If the person you are caring for breaks a promise to leave you assets in return for caregiving but you have a written contract—you are in luck. In most states, a written contract that meets the criteria I detailed in the previous section is considered valid whether it is part of the will or not.

If you don't have a written contract, and you find out that the person whom you cared for and who promised to leave you their estate left it all instead to the local museum or their distant cousin, then it will be difficult to claim what was promised to you. Every state, for example, requires that contracts that involve land (which includes houses on the land) must be in writing. As you can imagine, so many unwritten promises to leave an estate to caregivers involve a home or property. But land is so valuable that the law has an interest in reducing the chances of fraud when it is transferred from one person to another—making it that much harder for women caregivers to receive what they are so often promised in exchange for their sacrifices.

Many states also *require* that contracts involving promised inheritance be in writing to be enforceable. This can prevent you from enforcing an oral contract to receive property in exchange for caregiving. Take the case of Marie, whose grandmother asked her to move into her house with her children and care for her until her death.[14] In return, her grandmother promised to leave the house to Marie at her death as a home for her and her children, and Marie did move in and care for her grandmother until her death. After she died, it turned out that the grandmother had left the house to her daughter—Marie's mother—in her will instead of Marie. She had executed the will about twenty years before and had not changed it—who knows why? She was sick and dying, she forgot, she thought the promise was enough—we'll never know. But whatever the reason, after devoting herself full time to caring for her grandmother, Marie was left without what she had been promised—and with no place to live.

Marie stayed in the house with her children anyway—she had nowhere else to go. Four years later, Blanche—her mother, did I mention that?—sued to evict her from the house. Marie responded that it was hers because her grandmother had promised it to her and she had performed her part of the bargain.

Problem was, it wasn't in writing. Marie's state (Alaska) has a law saying that all contracts relating to inheritance must be in writing. The jury found in her favor anyway, because she had fulfilled her part. But Blanche appealed, and the Supreme Court of Alaska reversed, based on the inheritance contract rule.

So this isn't exactly a case of a wife caring for a husband and then getting cheated of the compensation she had been promised, but it's still a pretty typical case of the gender-based impact of these rules. Marie was the granddaughter, and while we don't know if there were other, male, grandchildren, it's most common that the person doing the caregiving is female—whether wife, daughter, or granddaughter. And so these rules about having the contract in writing—like all the other laws I discuss in this book—have a disproportionate impact on women.

As described in the opening story, the other huge challenge that you'll have to overcome is the "family member rule"—the concept that you can't expect to be paid by a family member you are caring for because it is your duty to do so. As with Hildegard's case, your claim that the person promised you assets in exchange for your caregiving might not carry much weight, especially if you admit you were taking care of the person because you love them or care for their well-being. But that's the biggest hurdle: most caregivers *do* love those they care for.

In some states, however, you might be able to get an oral contract (including one involving a house or land) enforced by relying on the legal doctrine that—even if there isn't a written contract—it would be unfair for you *not* to get the compensation you were promised because you actually performed your part of the deal.

That was the case of Brian and his father, John. After Brian's mother died, Brian helped his father build a house and lived with him in it for thirty years. On many occasions, John promised Brian that he would leave him his entire estate in exchange for Brian caring for him. Because of these promises, Brian stayed in the home with John, caring for him, paying many of his expenses, and even financing a lawsuit his father filed against the city.

In the last years of John's life, he became aggressive and paranoid, going as far as threatening to shoot Brian and blaming him for not winning his lawsuit. Brian moved out, but he continued to care for his father and pay his bills. Five years after Brian moved out, John committed suicide. Although he had originally executed a will in favor of Brian, John had changed the will in the last year of his life to disinherit him.

Though the law would normally have required a written contract that spelled out the promise Brian's father had made in exchange for Brian's caregiving, a California court ruled that it would be unfair for the executor of the estate to use the lack of a contract as a defense if it resulted in injustice—that is, denying Brian the benefit of the bargain he had carried out. In other words, Brian has to prove that he relied on his father's promise by caring for him and helping with the house, thus limiting the amount of energy Brian could spend on his own affairs.

Three states—Delaware, Maryland, and Virginia—will enforce oral contracts, like Brian's, to make wills. But even in these states, there are a couple of significant hurdles to proving that there was an agreement. First, you must present evidence that is extensive and detailed—in legal terms, "clear and convincing." This is the highest level of evidence that can be admitted in a civil case—a high bar to meet. Second, you must also prove that the deceased person promised you a *specific* item of property or amount of assets—a vague promise to "provide for" you or "take care of" you is not enough.

All states have rules that bar "an interested party"—in this case *you*, the person who is making a claim to the deceased person's estate—from testifying about anything the person said to her about the will. It's easy to understand the rationale for this rule: the dead person isn't there to refute what you say. So other people who have no interest in the inheritance would have to give evidence in support of your claim. States vary with respect to how much of this testimony they require.

As you see, it's possible to "get out from under" the requirement to present a written contract—but it's not easy. You must show that you performed your part of the oral contract to such an extent that to not enforce your agreement with the person you cared for would cause a serious injustice to you. In many states, you must also show that you expected to be paid for caregiving while you were doing it. That's a tall order, indeed.

YOU CAN SUE IF YOU'RE BEING HARASSED AT WORK FOR BEING A CAREGIVER

Although estate and property laws in general do not do enough to protect the wealth of women who give up so much to take care of those they love, some laws do protect caregivers in one significant way: by protecting them from discrimination at work.

Part of the reason women find it so hard to take care of loved ones and keep their jobs and careers on track is that employers so often have a bias against them. On top of the stress of caregiving, they have to deal with harassment at work and bosses who refuse to accommodate their need for flexible schedules—even if their performance stays the same. No wonder so many women quit their jobs. When women go part time to attend to their caregiving responsibilities, they often are overlooked for training, advancement, and promotion because they are seen as "not serious" about their careers.

The name for this type of discrimination is Family Responsibility Discrimination or FRD. It occurs when an employee suffers "adverse employment actions"—that is, they are fired, demoted, harassed, denied promotion, or retaliated against because of an employer's bias against family caregivers without regard for the employee's actual performance. Although there is no one federal law at this time that makes FRD illegal, there are many laws that prohibit FRD. For example, the Family and Medical Leave Act protects employees who have or need to take family leave to take care of a sick family member from being discriminated or retaliated against. [15]

Fortunately, the law has begun to recognize the injustice of these situations, and women have brought successful lawsuits on a number of grounds. Sixty-three local governments in twenty-two states have laws that make FRD a basis for a damages award. Even if you don't live in one of these cities, you may still have a case under a number of other laws if you are being harassed or discriminated against at work because of your caregiving responsibilities.

If you think you are being discriminated against at work for caregiving, first talk to the human resources department at your workplace, if there is one. Tell them about your situation, how much you want to do a good job at your work, and say that you feel you are being discriminated against because of your caregiving responsibilities and you know it is against the law. HR's job is to keep the company from getting sued, so they will likely try to fix the situation. If not, you should certainly consult an employment law attorney—but go to HR first. You'd have to try to remedy the situation this way before you could bring a lawsuit anyway.

If there isn't an HR department, or if they are unhelpful, consult an attorney experienced in workplace discrimination. There are also many online discussion boards where people exchange ideas and experiences and get recommendations. Start with work-lifelaw.org, a website based at the University of California's Hastings College of the Law.

The first line of defense against losing wealth because of caregiving is not to lose—or quit—your job and not to miss out on the professional advancement that would normally be available to you. Take the steps you can to head this off at the pass—the law in this area at least can be on your side!

PROTECT YOURSELF

Talk with all family members involved and get an agreement on who will give care, in what ways, and make sure everyone understands what the caregiver(s) will sacrifice in terms of wealth—income, investment, career advancement, promotions, overtime pay, pension, and social security—and agree on how the person will be compensated.

Remember, you are always best with a written contract. Once you have reached a consensus with family members, this may not be a difficult step to take. Explain to the person you are caring for how this will enable you to provide the care you want to give.

My hope is that this chapter will help you avoid the financial pitfalls of caregiving, encourage you to protect yourself by drafting a written contract with the person you are caring for, and to speak up if you feel you've been discriminated for your caregiving. Don't let caregiving lead to your impoverishment in later life. The sacrifices you are likely making will have serious financial consequences for you in later life. Protect yourself from them now.

6

DISINHERITED—THE FATE OF THE SURVIVING SPOUSE

Kathleen and Gilles met in 1999.[1] Both of them were divorced and had children from previous marriages. Still at their prime of their life—forty-five and forty years old respectively—they decided to get married after a short courtship. On July 3, 2000, Kathleen and Gilles exchanged vows in the state of Maryland where they lived. Their marriage, unfortunately, was brief. In early 2004, Gilles learned that he had lymphoma. Kathleen nursed him for several months while he went through chemotherapy, radiation treatment, and a stem-cell transplant. Although the stem cell transplant was successful and he was pronounced cancer free, he died suddenly in October of that year.

After his death in 2008, Kathleen found out that only a few months before dying, Gilles had transferred most of his estate—$422,000—into a trust for his daughter from a prior marriage, leaving Kathleen only the proceeds from his life insurance policy and a Toyota Highlander worth $22,000.

Maryland law guarantees a surviving spouse like Kathleen a percentage of the dead spouse's estate. So Kathleen filed a petition with the court, arguing that her share of Gilles's estate should be calculated by including in it the assets Gilles had transferred to the trust, since the transfer basically "emptied" his estate and left her with little to inherit. The court refused to do so, however, preferring not to question what it called Gilles's legitimate estate planning. It ruled that as long as Gilles had a legitimate reason for putting the assets into the trust—and leaving most of his assets to his daughter was a legitimate reason—Kathleen could not have access to it.

Most people think of marriage as a partnership—a joint venture or a mutual investment of effort and resources to build a life together that benefits both partners equally. You probably do too, even if you are not married at the moment. If marriage is an equal partnership, shouldn't the surviving spouse get half the estate when one of them dies? Should the spouse who dies first be able to disinherit the survivor, that is, leave that person out of his will, or transfer everything to other people outside of the will so she receives nothing, no matter how long they were married?

In Maryland, as in all other states, if a person dies without a will (and most Americans do[2]) or if a person attempts to leave his or her spouse out of the will or leave too little to him or her, the law guarantees the surviving spouse a share of the estate regardless of what the will says. (This is called an "elective share.") In this way, the law offers some protection to the surviving spouse from being disinherited. But this protection is limited: most states don't guarantee the survivor half of the estate but instead limit the amount a surviving partner can claim to one-third of the estate (and in some states this percentage can vary depending on whether there are surviving children as well). One-third doesn't seem like a fair share of a partnership, does it?

In a previous chapter, I discussed ways the law often fails to acknowledge the partnership nature of a marriage during divorce by not compensating the spouse who made sacrifices or contributed unpaid work to building that shared life. In this chapter, I explain how the law also fails to do so when a spouse dies. While inheritance laws offer some protection to a surviving spouse— statistically likely to be you, a woman—they deliver a subtle but nonetheless ruthless blow to women's ability to hold on to wealth they helped create by allowing spouses to disinherit their surviving spouses despite the law. I explore the many ways women are often de facto disinherited and offer recommendations for what you can do now to ensure it doesn't happen to you.

DISINHERITING WOMEN

To understand why inheritance laws disadvantage women, it's important to understand some basics of estate law—and to turn back in time to learn where those laws came from.

In an ideal world, everyone would die with a will in place. A will is a legal document that states clearly how you want to dispose of your estate, that is, to whom you want to leave your property and assets. Property or assets that pass by will are called the "probate estate" because wills are administered by the probate court.

Today, a lot of property doesn't pass to others through a will. Think about a joint bank account, for example. If you are married, you probably have one with your spouse. Should your spouse die, the account and money would belong to you and you alone. Or think about life insurance policies that require policy holders to name the person—the beneficiary—who will receive the insurance money when they die. Other property that doesn't pass through a will includes property held in joint tenancy. If the house you share with your spouse is held in joint tenancy, for example, the name on the deed will determine who gets it if your spouse dies. All the person named on the deed needs to do is show up at the registry of deeds with the death certificate, and, just like that, that person is the new owner. (It better be you on that deed!) These are some of the most common assets that do not pass under the will; instead, they pass according what is written in the instrument. They are called "nonprobate property" because they pass to the new owner without any contact with the probate court. The difference between probate and nonprobate property is crucial for spousal inheritance, as I explain later.

As I mentioned, most people who die in the United States, unfortunately, do so without a will, and often their surviving families have to go to court to settle their inheritance claims. Now, of those who do set up a will and are married—especially in a single long-term marriage—most leave all or a significant part of their estate to their spouse. But many people who are in a second or third marriage often prefer to leave all or most of their estate to someone else—most commonly, children from a previous relationship. And this is when surviving spouses often lose out unfairly.

How?

Earlier in the chapter, I shared that the laws in most states guarantee a portion (typically one-third) of the deceased person's estate to the surviving spouse if there's no will or if the will leaves too little to them. But it's important to note that these laws guarantee a portion of the *probate estate*. By limiting the "pot" from which the survivor takes his or her share to just the probate estate, they create a loophole: all a spouse has to do before death is title all or much of his or her property and assets in a way that makes it "nonprobate." Magically, those assets disappear from the probate estate as far as the surviving spouse is concerned—and now the surviving spouse cannot even claim a portion of them.

You might be asking yourself, why, if our current view of marriage is that of an equal partnership, don't our laws guarantee the survivor half of the deceased person's estate? Why do most states not only limit the share of a deceased person's estate that the surviving spouse can claim to one-third but also allow people to divert most or all of their assets away from the surviving spouse, even if the marriage was long term?

The answer is simple: history—and the lack of incentive to change it.

The idea that a surviving spouse can only claim one-third of their dead spouse's estate comes from medieval English law (yep, back to the Middle Ages again) brought into the colonies by settlers. Women in those days were not allowed to inherit property or assets except for whatever they brought into the marriage.[3] English law gave the surviving widow one-third of her dead husband's property for her life (the other two-thirds went directly to the oldest make heir). The widow had a right to live there for the rest of her life, but she did not have the right to sell it or leave it to her heirs; the land she had been allowed to live on for her life went back to her husband's heirs (usually the eldest male).

Today, inheritance laws acknowledge women's rights to own and inherit property. But they still don't reflect most people's views of marriage as an equal partnership or treat women fairly. They might give the appearance of being fair to women and men equally. After all, today's laws—such as the right to receive one-third of the deceased spouse's estate regardless of what is in the will—apply to male and female surviving spouses equally. But in practice, these laws statistically disadvantage women for two reasons. First, on average women are more likely to survive their husbands. Though scientists debate the reasons, women outlive men in every society on earth, including the United States.[4] Second, as I've argued in other chapters, women are much more likely to be financially dependent or have accumulated less wealth as a result of taking a larger share of household, child-rearing, and caregiving responsibilities.

Since men typically die before their (usually) less wealthy wives, inheritance laws don't affect their financial status nearly as much. When men outlive their wives, since their wives don't have as much wealth as they do in the first place, these laws don't affect their financial status as they do women. But women who outlive their husbands suffer financially when they are not able to receive an equitable share of the wealth they helped to create.

Is there any doubt that if the statistics were reversed and men on average lived longer than their wives that the laws would be more equitable to ensure that men could always claim *half* an interest in their dead wives' estate (regardless of how little that would be)? Since that is not the case—and since most lawmakers are men today—there's no incentive to change the law to reflect the idea that marriage is a partnership of equals. In fact, there might be a *disincentive* to change. Male lawmakers are more likely to see inheritance laws from the perspective of the man who will likely die first. Indeed, they may prefer not to change laws that allow them to leave their estate to someone other than their surviving spouse if they wish.

HOW TO MAGICALLY REDUCE THE POT—AND THE SURVIVING SPOUSE'S ELECTIVE SHARE

If your spouse dies and has left you little or nothing in his will, you can choose to instead claim your elective share—the portion of your spouse's estate the laws of your state guarantee you. As I explained, in most states, the elective share is calculated based only on the deceased spouse's *probate estate*. (And this is only after your deceased spouse's creditors have been paid. In most states, your share gets taken from what's left—if any.) But there are many ways spouses can transfer assets to nonprobate property, effectively disinheriting their surviving spouses by reducing the pot from which her elective share is calculated. Perhaps the most common ways are by diverting assets to a trust, setting up "pay-on-death" accounts, and gifting money away.

Don't Trust the Trust

A trust is a way to give money—or any kind of assets—to someone (the trustee) to hold and manage for someone else (the beneficiary). The trustee distributes the money to the beneficiary according to the terms of the trust. Under certain circumstances, the trustee and beneficiary can be the same person—so, in effect, one can set up a trust that allows individuals to pay money to themselves whenever they want. The fact that the assets are in a trust makes absolutely no difference to their day-to-day lives. But the money in the trust is no longer in the "probate estate." Many married couples have trusts in which both partners are trustees. In many states, however, the spouse who dies first—likely the husband—can, while alive, create a trust, transfer assets to it, and leave the assets in the trust to anyone he wishes to, including someone who is not his surviving spouse.

That's what happened in Vanya's case.[5]

George and Vanya were married for twenty-six years until George's death. Although they had no children together, they each had children from prior marriages. During much of the marriage, George and Vanya ran two businesses: a jewelry store and an import-export business. After being married for sixteen years, they decided to close the jewelry store, and both of them worked in the import-export company until a year before George's death.

Two years before he died, George put all the stock from the import-export business into a trust with himself and his two daughters from his previous marriage as the beneficiaries. While he was alive, he drew income from this trust and retained the right to revoke the trust and to withdraw assets from it. When George died, Vanya learned that the assets in the trust were to be divided between his daughters—none were to go to Vanya, even though she had worked at the import-export business for all twenty-six years of their marriage and had worked there exclusively since they closed the jewelry store.

Vanya brought suit, claiming that she should be able to take her third of George's estate from the trust assets because, for all intents and purposes, he had complete control of the assets during his life—he could spend the money, give it away, and even dissolve the trust. There was in substance no difference between the assets being in trust and being in George's bank account. But the court held that the mere fact that the money was in a trust—the mere fact that he had signed some documents that had no effect on how he could use the money—meant that they were no longer probate property and, therefore, out of Vanya's reach as a surviving spouse.

Now, no one would say George shouldn't have the right to leave something to his daughters from his prior marriage. But was it fair for him to leave them all of the assets of a business he built jointly with Vanya over many years, while cutting Vanya out completely? George and Vanya's marriage was a literal partnership—a business partnership. She worked hard to create wealth for both of them via their businesses. It's unfair for the law to allow George to cheat her out of the fruits of her labor by using the technicality of a trust.

Occasionally, a court will invalidate a trust if it seems clear that the only reason the spouse created it was to cheat his surviving spouse out of her share of the estate. But this intent is very hard to prove: if there was any other possible legitimate reason for the creation of the trust, the trust will be considered valid. Of course, there's almost always a way to argue that there was *some* legitimate reason for the creation of a trust. This is what Kathleen, the surviving spouse in the chapter's opening story, found when her husband left most of his assets in trust for his daughter, leaving Kathleen with a small part of the estate. In her case, as in Vanya's, leaving *all* your assets to children from a prior marriage is considered a legitimate reason.

Some states don't even care if a trust *was* set up with an intent to cheat the surviving spouse. They consider a trust untouchable no matter what. Nancy found this out the hard way.[6] Her husband of thirty-eight years, Milton, created a revocable living trust two years prior to his death, putting most of his assets, including the couple's residence, into it. When he died, Milton had about $7 million in assets, of which only $247,386 passed through probate. Instead, he left Nancy the income from a trust and the right to live in the residence for her life (just as in the Middle Ages!). After she died, the remaining assets in the trust including the residence would pass to charity.

Nancy claimed that the trust should be ignored because its sole purpose was to deprive her of her legally guaranteed share of the estate. The court found no remedy, however; it said that it could not undo the transfer even if it was done "with the specific intent to diminish or eliminate a surviving spouse's statutory elective share." (The court, though, did admit to being "troubled" by the result.)

Then there are states like Illinois. Illinois law explicitly affirms the right of a spouse to cheat his surviving spouse: it provides that a person may "dispose of his property during his lifetime in any manner he sees fit . . . even though the transfer is for the precise purpose of minimizing or defeating the statutory marital interests of the spouse in the property conveyed." Notice that the law refers to "his property"—it's pretty clear who the other spouse is, isn't it? And whose "interests" are being "defeated"?

Finally, if your spouse is the beneficiary of a trust created for him by someone else, it will likely not be counted as part of his estate for purposes of your share—even if he has what amounts to full ownership rights in the money—that is, he can withdraw as much as he wants anytime for any purpose.

For example: Nancy and Paul married in 1995.[7] Paul was the beneficiary of a trust created for him by his father in 1983. The terms of the trust allowed the trustees to pay out any amount to Paul they thought he might want or need. The terms also provided that after Paul reached the age of twenty-five, he could withdraw certain percentages of the trust assets in increasing amounts until, at age forty-seven, he could withdraw all the money from the trust and terminate it. In 2010, Paul filed for divorce. By this time Paul had reached the age when he could withdraw up to 75 percent of the trust money. In March 2011, the trustees of the trust—who included Paul's brother—transferred the assets of the trust to a new trust that—lo and behold!—had new terms that no longer allowed Paul to withdraw any assets.

This was clearly an attempt to remove the trust assets from Paul's control so that a court would not count them as marital assets and divide them between him and Nancy. (After a fifteen-year marriage, a court would have done its best to make a fair division of the property Paul and Nancy owned.) What Paul's brother did was the equivalent of him saying to Paul, "Hey, you're getting divorced and a court might share your property with your wife. How about you give it to me and then you can say it's not yours—that way, a court can't give her any. Then I'll give it back to you."

A court would have seen through *that* little trick in no time. But because this property was in trust, the court got distracted by the question of whether the trustees were allowed to move the assets to a new trust and decided that, under Massachusetts law, they could. The judges completely ignored the pretty obvious fact that this whole transaction was meant to make sure Nancy didn't get property she would have likely have received in divorce court—because remember, the fact that the money was in a trust was meaningless. Paul had access to most of it free and clear with no restrictions whatsoever. And do you have any doubt that the trustee-brother will hesitate a second before handing it all back to him the minute the divorce is final?

Or take the case of George and Jean.[8] They were married for more than thirty years, and for that whole time they lived in an apartment building that was held in a trust created by George's mother to benefit her family. The trust also contained a bank account. The terms of the trust gave George the ability to withdraw as much money as he wanted from the bank account, to live on the rents from the tenants, and to give the property to anyone he wanted in his will. When George died, he left Jean nothing in his will. Jean claimed her elective share and argued that under Massachusetts law the trust should be considered part of George's estate and thus be counted when calculating her share. After all, for all intents and purposes, the property in the trust belonged to George: he could use it, give it away, or leave it to anyone he wanted in his will. He had complete control over those assets; the trust form didn't really mean anything.

And that's the point of the elective share—it's meant to protect the surviving spouse from being disinherited if the other spouse cuts her out of his will. This is what happened here. George actually had a lot of property—he just didn't leave any of it to Jean.

But the court saw things differently. It got stuck on the technicality that the assets were in a trust created by someone else. Massachusetts law stated that the surviving spouse's elective share was to be taken out of her husband's "estate," and the court decided that this meant "probate estate." Remember the difference between probate and nonprobate I explained earlier? Although the Massachusetts law didn't say this, the court decided on its own that the term "estate" meant just the assets that passed through George's will and that those were the only assets that "counted" for purposes of calculating Jean's share.

Since the trust assets were the bulk of what George owned, this didn't leave much for Jean. The decision in this case seems to ignore the point of the elective share—to give the survivor a fair share of the assets her spouse owned at death so she can continue to benefit from the marital partnership after the death of the spouse. After all, the trust assets were what Jean and George lived on during their marriage.

Unfortunately, this decision is typical. So that's the story with trusts. If your husband left those assets to you, you're in luck. If not, the assets in the trust are nonprobate property in many states and won't be counted to calculate your elective share of the estate.

By the way, it's worth noting that Jean would have been better off property-wise if she had divorced George instead of staying married until he died. In that case, the trust assets would likely have been considered marital property to be divided between them. Actually, the court noted this odd discrepancy but seemed untroubled by the perverse results—give a spouse who divorces her husband a fairer share of the property than she gets if she stays with him until he dies.

Pay on Death

The trust is not the only form of "nonprobate transfer"—a way to give someone your property at death without using a will—that can be used to deplete the surviving spouse's "pot." Other examples include so-called pay-on-death accounts: these are bank accounts that specify who will get the money in the account when the primary account holder dies. The transfer typically avoids probate, and thus many states exclude them from the reach of the survivor's elective share. The same is often true of beneficiary designations on retirement accounts. If your spouse holds investments in a brokerage account to which you don't have what's

called joint ownership, then he can designate anyone else he de-
sires to receive the assets in the account upon his death.

That's what happened to Karen, who survived her husband
Howard.[9] Karen inherited the house they lived in, but Howard
left everything else to his daughters and stepson. Karen decided to
file for her elective share and argued that a checking account, a
CD, and an annuity, together worth about $110,000, were part of
Howard's estate and should be counted when calculating her elective share.

The problem was, these assets passed automatically at Howard's death to the beneficiary listed on the form. Guess what this
means? You got it, right? They didn't pass by will and therefore
were not part of Howard's estate for purpose of Karen's elective
share. So that's another pretty easy way to shrink the pot, isn't it?
Just make sure all your assets—almost any asset can be treated this
way—pass to the named beneficiary rather than under your will.
And hey, presto—it disappears!

Giving Away the Inheritance

Another very simple way to deplete an estate prior to death—and
in effect reduce the elective share of a surviving spouse—is to give
generous gifts to children from prior marriages, friends, business
associates, or anyone at all. For the purpose of calculating the
elective share, a few states include gifts made within two years of
death in the elective share pot, but many ignore them entirely. If
your spouse has enough money that he does not have to worry
about paying his expenses, then gifting large sums is an easy way to
reduce the amount of his estate.

Here's the case of Joan and her husband, Sheldon.[10] Shortly
before his death, Sheldon, who was on the outs with Joan, transferred a lot of property to various people other than her—various
friends and business partners. Specifically, he transferred most of
his interest in land and buildings, his shares in a corporation, his
right to collect several mortgages, and a bank account. Sheldon got

no payment for these transfers—they were just gifts. Joan, who got nothing under Sheldon's will, claimed her share of his estate under state law. She also insisted that the assets he had gifted to his friends should be counted as part of his estate—as part of the pot from which her share would be taken. This seems fair, doesn't it? After all, what else was Sheldon trying to do by giving away all his property shortly before he died besides make sure Joan didn't get it? Should the law allow a husband to do this just because he's mad at his wife—or likes other people better? Think about it: he's sick and knows he's going to die within a few months or maybe a year; he has enough for what he needs until then and wants to keep his surviving spouse from inheriting the rest. Under those circumstances, it's pretty easy for him to just give it away to other people—and hey, presto, no estate!

But is this fair? If marriage is a partnership, it doesn't really seem to be fair, does it? After all, if you believe in marriage as a partnership, the assets that Sheldon got title to during marriage were product of the partnership, right? Even if she stayed home and kept house and raised kids, her labor was what enabled him to devote himself to his businesses. So what right does he have to give it all away when he knows he's dying just so she can't get her share?

Well, the court didn't see it that way, even though it agreed that Sheldon probably made the transfers intending to cheat Joan out of the estate. That leaves a pretty big loophole in the elective share, doesn't it?

Without a doubt, elective share law is better than nothing; it offers some protections. But the fact that this elective share can so easily be intentionally reduced suggests that it does not go far enough to protect the interests of surviving spouses—usually women. Elective share laws might even prevent you from leaving property to your children. To claim an elective share, you must file a claim for it with the probate court. But if you pass away before you have a chance to file this claim—say, something unexpected happens, or you are close in age to your husband and don't survive him by long enough to decide what to do about the elective share—in most states, the elective share is lost.

The right to leave your assets and property to those you choose—the right to "devise"—is an important property right everyone has. The Supreme Court has even called it a fundamental right—one of the most important kinds of rights, such as the right to marry or to have children. If you believe that marriage is a partnership, and that you own a share of the assets of that partnership, your share of your spouse's estate should be yours to leave to your heirs. Why should your death change that? It's not as if your other property disappears when you die. But your share of marital partnership property does. This is yet another example of the law's refusal to recognize what most people believe: that marriage is a joint venture to which both spouses contribute and from which they both deserve the profits.

Life Insurance

Here's yet another way to disinherit your spouse (yes, the list goes on and on): say you don't have much in the way of money or property. You can probably still afford a life insurance policy with a large payout; depending on your age and health, you can probably get one for a pretty modest monthly rate. Or if you really want to siphon money from your estate, you can pay more and get a really big payout—for someone other than your surviving spouse.

Joint Bank Accounts

Another way a spouse can deplete the estate in many states is by using joint ownership of bank accounts or property. When an asset is held jointly, it passes at the death of the first of the joint owners to the other joint owner. So it doesn't go through probate; and as explained before, many states don't count assets as part of the survivor's share unless they go through probate.

As an illustration, take the case of Vida and Francis.[11] Francis died, leaving his surviving spouse, Vida, and no children. The value of Francis's estate was about $123,000, but Vida got less than $15,000. That's because almost $100,000 of his assets were in joint bank accounts with a joint owner other than Vida. So all the money in the accounts passed outside of probate to the other owner, and Vida was left with a tiny fraction of the estate. So she chose to take her share under state law rather than what was left to her in the will and argued that the money in the joint accounts should be part of the pot.

The court disagreed. It rejected Vida's argument that keeping the money in the joint accounts out of her share was bad policy, since it made it easy for a spouse to disinherit his surviving spouse. But this is really as unfair as all the other scenarios we've discussed, isn't it? It's just too easy in many states to shrink the pot—and leave the surviving spouse with nothing.

SUPPORT, NOT PARTNERSHIP

At least being guaranteed a share of the estate, even if it's only a third, is something, right? If the estate hasn't been completely depleted by creditors' claims, and if its assets weren't siphoned off into a trust benefiting someone else, at least you get a share of it, right? Well, maybe. In some states such as South Dakota, there's a catch: these states allow for the surviving spouse's elective share to be satisfied by something called a "life estate in property" or a "life interest in trust." Connecticut actually *limits* your share to a life estate.[12]

A life estate means that, rather than owning property outright, you are a "temporary owner" who can live in and even rent out the property and generate income from it but can't sell it, give it to someone, or leave it to your heirs after your death. The property instead stays in a trust until your death; then it is transferred to whatever beneficiary your spouse might have designated. A "life interest in a trust" is similar: it means that you do not get access to the assets in the trust, but rather all you have a right to is the income from the trust, which the trustee will distribute to you at whatever intervals the trust documents require.

A life estate or life interest provides you with support during your lifetime. And while there are good uses of it in estate planning, it often undermines the very idea of partnership. After all, the wealth and assets that you helped acquire during your marriage are not being equally shared with you. Having the right to the income from a trust or being a temporary owner of a property is very different from owning those assets outright. You can't control the actual assets—the real wealth—at all. For example, you can't sell the property or use any of the money funding the trust unless the trust allows you to dip into it under certain circumstances. Even then, the trustee has the final say over what you can get. The capital—the real wealth—stays in the trust. And you can't decide what happens to that capital, that wealth, when you die: the person who set up the trust, your spouse in the scenario we are focused on here, decides whom he wants the trust assets to go to after your death.

In fact, there is a special kind of trust designed specifically for spouses that die first to provide an income for the surviving spouse during her life but transfer the actual assets to someone else after her death: the QTIP (Qualified Terminable Interest Property) trust.

Why is a QTIP special and a little different than just leaving someone a life interest in a property or trust? It creates a loophole for spouses who want to leave their spouses with little to no property *but still get the marital deduction for the whole amount*. To understand how a QTIP trust works and why it benefits the spouse who dies first (and sets the trust)—typically men—you'll need to understand some of the basics of estate or inheritance taxes.

Normally, when someone dies with a large estate, their estate is taxed by the federal government if it is over a certain amount.[13] But there's an exemption: whatever a spouse leaves the surviving spouse is tax free. This is one instance in which marital partnership is actually acknowledged by our tax laws. The logic behind this tax exemption is that property and assets in a marriage belong to both spouses and are subject to their joint decision making; assets owned by either spouse are really "their" assets and they have joint control over them. Because it belongs to both of them, transferring those assets to the surviving spouse after one of them dies is not a real transfer and therefore should not be taxed.

The catch: Up until 1981, you really had to leave your estate to the surviving spouse. If a spouse left property to both the surviving spouse and, say, to his son from a previous marriage, the estate paid tax on whatever part the son got. And if a spouse left property in trust with income for life to his surviving spouse—that life interest I introduced you to earlier—and the assets of the trust to his son after her death, the estate paid taxes on the part left to his son. Back then, if a spouse didn't want to leave the surviving spouse full control of his property and assets, he didn't get the deduction.

This rule was inconvenient if a husband wanted to leave a lot of property to someone other than his surviving spouse—typically children from a prior marriage—but didn't want to pay taxes on it. Or if he did not think women could handle money. Or if he thought all his surviving spouse deserved was support, not control over their assets. So Congress helpfully passed a bill in 1981 allowing for the QTIP trust.

Under the QTIP provision, the first spouse to pass away can leave the survivor income for life from a trust, leave the assets in the trust—the much larger amount—to anyone he wants after the surviving spouse's death, and *still get a marital deduction on all the estate*. But forget about joint control—now the deceased spouse has made the decision about who really gets the assets in the end.

This is bad enough: the decedent spouse gets a large marital property tax deduction for money that isn't marital—because the surviving spouse never gets to own it. Then, in 1996, after the QTIP trust had been law for several years, the tax court made it even more degrading—and harmful—to women. Here's the scenario: When Willis died in 1987, he made his surviving spouse, Alice, the beneficiary of a QTIP trust—maybe.[14] The trouble was, Willis left it up to the executor of his estate, his son Richard, to decide whether to fund the marital trust or not. But he still claimed the marital deduction for whatever amount Richard decided to put into the trust. Notice what happened here: Willis wanted the marital deduction for as much of his estate as was possible. But he didn't want his widow to have complete control of the assets either, despite calling them "marital" for tax purposes—so far, so good. We knew this was possible under the QTIP legislation. But what Willis wanted was to get the marital deduction even if his widow Alice *had no control over whether the trust was set up or not.* The decision was completely out of her hands; it was up to her son.

The IRS, unsurprisingly, objected on the grounds that there should not be a marital deduction when the surviving spouse had no control whatsoever over the fate of the property. Indeed, she had no idea, at the date of her husband's death, what her property rights were; she would now have to wait until someone else decided for her. But the tax court ruled in the estate's favor, symbolically snapping the last thread connecting the marital deduction to any notion of truly marital property.

This case was decided several years ago, but this remains the law today. So now the first spouse to pass doesn't need to be the one to set up a QTIP trust. The executor of the deceased spouse's estate—who doesn't have to be the surviving spouse—can make the decision that the estate will pass in the form of a QTIP trust *after* the first spouse dies. And there's no requirement that the surviving spouse agree to the choice of a QTIP trust. It doesn't matter if she would rather take the property outright; if she is not the executor of her dead husband's estate, it's not up to her.

Could this law possibly be explained by the fact that everyone involved in its drafting and enactment was thinking of the surviving spouse as the woman, which is statistically likely to be the case? It is not a surprise that, while the final legislation that made QTIP trust possible was written in gender-neutral language, the original deliberations and proposals all use examples of a female surviving spouse.[15] If Congress viewed marriage as a partnership of equals, they probably would not have enacted rules that allowed marital deductions for property totally controlled by one spouse. This is yet another way our inheritance laws often fails to recognize marriage as a partnership and, in thus failing, disinherits women.

THE PITFALLS OF EMPLOYER-OFFERED BENEFIT PLANS

There's one final way in which our legal system fails to protect women from being disinherited—and it comes from an unexpected federal law: ERISA, the Employee Retirement Income Security Act.

ERISA controls and regulates any kind of benefit plans offered by employers, including 401(k), 403(b), group life insurance, or pensions. This federal law was adopted to address employer fraud and embezzlement of pension funds; its goal was to create an overarching, national set of standard procedures that would enforce strict regulation of pensions and ensure that workers weren't cheated out of their retirement money.

Here's the problem: Most states have laws stating that when a couple divorces, bequests the spouses made for each other are automatically revoked by law. For example, if a person lists their spouse as beneficiary in their will, when they are divorced, that beneficiary designation is revoked automatically. Should the person die, the now ex-spouse will not receive the proceeds of the 401(k). Makes sense, right? It seems fair to assume that spouses who got divorced wouldn't want to benefit each other at death.

But federal law trumps state law. Under ERISA, the last person listed in the plan's documents as beneficiary receives the proceeds of that plan. The Supreme Court has ruled that this applies even if state laws revoke bequests to divorced spouses. So, if a person listed his spouse as beneficiary of his 401(k) account, then got divorced and failed to change the beneficiary designation on his 401(k) plan in the exact way ERISA requires, then his surviving ex-spouse would still get the proceeds of 401(k). This doesn't seem like what the person would have wanted, which is why state laws prevent it from happening. But ERISA overrules state laws, and it didn't occur to the drafters of ERISA to address this situation.

Now imagine that you married this person who got divorced but never got around to changing his 401(k) plan documents to remove his ex-wife as beneficiary and list you instead. Imagine that he was married to his first wife for only two years, and by his death you and he have been married for ten years. You would end up without a retirement benefit that is rightfully yours as the surviving spouse. Is it fair that his ex-spouse, not you, his current wife, gets to keep the wealth that you helped create?

Unfortunately, many people don't get around to changing the beneficiary designations of their retirement and life insurance accounts after divorce, even if their lawyer reminds them to. Most people take a few years to recover emotionally from the end of their marriage. During this time, they often aren't psychologically ready to do all the paperwork around finances. If a recently divorced person dies during this vulnerable time, they may well have a will or pension plan that names the now-divorced spouse as beneficiary.

Here's another problem with ERISA: it might compromise your ability to leave your rightful share of a retirement benefit or pension to whomever you decide when you die. That's precisely what happened to Dorothy.

Isaac and Dorothy were married for thirty-six years, during which time they lived in Louisiana, a community property state. They had three sons together. During that time, Isaac worked for South Central Bell, which provided him with several pension benefits (all governed by ERISA). In 1979, Dorothy died, and a year later Isaac married Sandra, to whom he stayed married until his death in 1989. When Isaac retired in 1985, he received a lump-sum payment of $151,628 from the Bell South Central Savings Plan, shares of AT&T stock, and a monthly annuity payment. He rolled the lump sum over into an IRA, which he left untouched until his death, by which time it was worth more than $180,000. When Isaac died, he left everything to Sandra.

The problem was that Dorothy had left her estate to her and Isaac's three sons. And according to her will, that estate included her share of Isaac's monthly annuity benefits, which she would have been entitled to if she had survived him. Two of the sons brought suit against Sandra, claiming that under Louisiana community property law, Dorothy had a right to an equal share of the pension payments (remember, the lump sum had already been paid out to Isaac, so ERISA no longer applied to it) and, if she died before Isaac, the right to leave her share to whomever she wished—in this case, them, the couple's sons. The trial court and the intermediate appeals court agreed and ruled for the sons. But the Supreme Court reversed, ruling that ERISA trumped even state community property law. [16]

Granted, Dorothy was not an impoverished widow. She wasn't cheated out of her community property while she was alive, and if she had divorced or outlived Isaac, she would have had a share of the ERISA plan benefits. But because she died before he did, she was cheated out of a very important aspect of property ownership—the right to pass it on to her heirs or anyone else she chose.

This is another case that might seem old and out of date. But it isn't; once this was decided, it became the law and determines property outcomes today. There are no more recent cases because no lawyer would agree to bring one: the outcome is a foregone conclusion. Dorothy's case established that the law often doesn't take women's property ownership seriously enough to give them all of the aspects of it that we take for granted.

It's worth noting that, had Isaac died before Dorothy, she would have continued to receive her share of the annuity being paid to him after his retirement (under ERISA called "survivor benefits"). But the lump sum that he got when he retired from Bell South Central Savings Plan would have become part of his estate for him to pass on to his heirs or anyone he wished to. The lump sum is payable to the working spouse alone, while the annuity is shared by both spouses. The working spouse can leave the lump sum to anyone he wants because it is his sole property, but the annuity is supposed to be the property of both spouses. Of course, this arrangement would benefit any woman who has an ERISA pension plan as well—ERISA treats the sexes equally. But here is the problem: ERISA rules have a disproportionate negative effect on women because men are more likely to have the kind of jobs with ERISA-covered plans—meaning, basically, higher-paying, skilled jobs.[17]

In making the lump-sum payment to the employed spouse alone, ERISA, like all the other laws we've been looking at, fails to recognize that marriage is a partnership. If it did, it would recognize that all the benefits accrued in an ERISA plan by an individual belong to him and his spouse equally since both spouses contribute equally to that individual's ability to go to work every day. In failing to do so, it often cheats women of wealth they helped accrue.

ANOTHER WAY FEDERAL LAW CHEATS WOMEN

One way to look at the ERISA case above is to see it as a way the courts have allowed federal law to trump state law protections for spousal property. Basically, in the above case, the Supreme Court set aside state community property law and made it inapplicable to ERISA-covered pension benefits, even though the couple lived in a community property state and had every reason to expect that their assets would be equally owned under its laws.

There's another example of the Supreme Court deciding to trump state property law meant to protect a surviving spouses. It has to do with the ownership of the marital home. About twenty-five states allow married couples—and only married couples—to own their home in a legal form called "tenancy by the entirety." This form of ownership was designed to protect the surviving spouse from losing her home due to her husband's debts. This is how it works: Normally, when a person reneges on a debt, the person they owe money to can file a lien against their property—and collect from their estate when they die. So, for example, if your husband fails to pay $100,000 of medical bills, the hospital can go to court and put a lien on his property. This means that when he sells it, the hospital gets its money, and at the very latest, it can collect that money from the property he leaves behind. This obviously reduces the amount the surviving spouse will receive when he dies. Tenancy by the entirety was meant to protect the couple's home from being subject to the debts of the first spouse to die—and thus to prevent the survivor from having to sell it to pay off such debt.

In a tenancy by the entirety, when one of the joint owners—husband or wife—dies, the interest they have in the home simply disappears, and the property belongs to the survivor, free and clear of any debt the other spouse might have had. In the above example, the hospital could collect the money owed them from any other assets the husband left behind—cars, bank accounts, and so forth—but the house would be off limits. This protects you, the surviving spouse, from losing your home if your husband left significant debt.

This all seems like a good idea, right? It seems to comport with all the ideas we've been discussing of protecting the surviving spouse—likely the wife—from impoverishment and making sure she can continue to live on the fruits of the marital partnership after the husband passes away. And that's exactly why so many states put it in place.

Then, in 2002, along came *United States v. Craft*.[18] In 1972, Don and Sandra bought a home in Grand Rapids, Michigan, for $48,000 and titled the house as a tenancy by the entirety in both their names. Don—a lawyer, I'm sorry to say—decided not to file income tax returns from 1979 to 1986. The IRS, as is the procedure in these situations, prepared substitute returns for him, and assesses a deficiency of $482,446. Don still didn't pay, and the IRS filed a tax lien against his property in 1989. Don and Sandra took Don's name off the deed and titled the house in Sandra's alone. Sandra then tried to sell the house, but when the buyers discovered the lien, they backed out (who wants to buy property with a federal lien on it?). Sandra filed a petition in federal court to have the lien removed, arguing that the lien had never attached to the property because it had been held in tenancy by the entirety, and then by her alone. She reminded the court that one spouse's debts cannot attach to property titled this way. And that was true—under state law.

Don died in 1998. The case went to the Supreme Court, which ruled that as a matter of federal law, one spouse's debts could cause a lien to attach to the home, even though it was held in tenancy by the entirety. This completely contradicted the state law. It meant that when Sandra sold the house, she would have to pay half the proceeds to the IRS to cover her now-deceased husband's taxes. Notice that the IRS filed the lien while the home was still held by Don and Sandra in a tenancy by the entirety. There is no doubt that under state law, none of Don's creditors would have been able to file a lien against the home. The Supreme Court ignored state law and basically made up a rule of federal property law, even though property is supposed to be governed by state law.

Think about the implications of this for a minute. Suppose Don and Sandra had the kind of relationship where the husband manages the family finances and the wife doesn't really concern herself with them—or isn't allowed to. This kind of gender relationship was probably more common in the seventies than it is today, but it's still not unusual today (what about your household?). What if Sandra trusted Don and just assumed he paid his taxes? (Would you know if your husband wasn't paying the taxes?) Then, she wakes up one day and finds out she can't sell the house because there's a tax lien on it—and then he dies, leaving her with the burdened property. This is exactly the scenario that state law was trying to prevent by protecting the marital home against one spouse's debt.

Do you think my picture of Sandra the housewife who naively trusted her husband is silly and out of date? Would it surprise you to learn that a very similar thing happened to my mother, a university professor with a PhD who worked full time and wrote numerous books and articles? It wasn't that she was oblivious to family finances, but she and my dad divided the tasks so that my mother paid the bills and balanced the checkbook, and my dad did the investing—and filed the taxes. Well, my dad really hated paying taxes, and my mom found out after he died that he had pulled all sorts of shenanigans in the family returns. By the time the IRS caught up to it all, my dad was gone and my mom was taken completely by surprise. The moral is, it could happen to you—and affect your financial well-being when you are older and retired.

There's nothing you can do about the Supreme Court ruling, but you can be aware of its pitfalls. And, as I keep saying, keep your nose in the family finances!

THE DANGERS OF NOT BEING INVOLVED IN ESTATE PLANNING

Before I end the chapter with recommendations for how you can protect yourself from being in essence disinherited, I want to share this final story to illustrate how often we women unwittingly help the men in our lives cheat us from our wealth. All too often we—still!—are a bit too likely to cede tax and financial planning to our male partners. By being uninformed or unreasonably trusting, we are not looking out for interests as we should.

Seventeen months before husband Emil's death, Lois and Emil met with an attorney to prepare an estate plan.[19] The attorney drew up wills and a living trust for each of them, and he also drew up four deeds: two of them conveying land to Lois's trust and two of them conveying land to Emil's trust. The land conveyed to Emil's trust was worth $2,529,460.

When Emil died a year and a half later, Lois filed a petition for an elective share and argued that the land conveyed to Emil's trust should be included in the estate for the purpose of calculating her share. Lois didn't argue that she had been tricked or pressured into signing the deeds for the land; she simply hadn't realized that transferring the deeds to Emil's trust would have any effect on what she would receive when he died. After all, transferring the land into Emil's living trust made no difference to how they used it—it was a mere formality. And because it was a living trust, Emil could have revoked it at any time by signing another piece of paper, transferring the land back to the couple's joint ownership.

The trial court agreed that just because Lois had signed the deed didn't mean that the land shouldn't be part of the estate from which she claimed her elective share. It noted that "although [Lois] signed warranty deeds conveying the real estate to [the trust], [Emil] retained the power to revoke the trust and enjoy the benefits from the income of this trust during his lifetime. . . . [Emil] effectively retained possession and enjoyment and right to the income from the property." In other words, this was not a real transfer that removed property from the estate; it was more of a sham that had no effect on Emil's estate or assets. But the Supreme Court of Nebraska reversed. It said that the rights Emil kept over the property—the exact same rights as an outright owner—didn't matter; it didn't matter that the land remained in Emil's possession and control. The only thing that mattered was that Lois signed the deeds.

It's impossible to know what Lois was thinking or what she knew when she signed the deeds. And it's impossible to know what the lawyer or her husband told her—or didn't tell her—about them. But it clearly never occurred to Lois that she was depleting the assets she stood to inherit from her husband's estate. Her lawyer—and he was her lawyer every bit as he was Emil's lawyer—should have explained that to Lois. And Lois should have asked how the deeds would affect her future after her husband's death.

Remember: When someone tells you something in the law is a "mere formality" or "technicality," it's probably a lot more—and it may be something that can harm you. Lois believed it when her husband and the lawyer told her that signing the deeds was a "mere formality," and look where it got her.

PROTECT YOURSELF

As one law professor put it, "What person would enter a business or joint venture if the only liquidation rule is that a court will have discretion to make any order it thinks fit with regard to the money and property?"[20] So why would you enter the partnership of marriage that way?

It's too late for Lois and the other women profiled in this chapter who were cheated out of their rightful inheritance. But it's not too late for you. Next, I'll offer some clear advice on what you can do today to prevent some of the scenarios described in this chapter from happening to you.

If you are married but have your own separate wealth, you may not be worried about being disinherited when your spouse passes away. If you don't, the following questions will help you figure out whether you are at risk of spousal disinheritance:

- Are you married to someone who is in a second or third marriage and who has children from any of those previous relationships?
- Does your spouse own property (real estate, bank accounts) jointly with other people besides you, such as children from prior marriages, siblings, or an ex-spouse?
- Do you lack sufficient assets of your own to maintain your lifestyle if you should outlive your spouse?
- Are you confident that you are aware of all the assets your spouse owns, or do you think it's possible he may have some you don't know about?
- Is your spouse secretive about his assets or wealth?

If the answer to any of these questions is "yes" or "maybe," you need to think about how to protect yourself. Here are some suggestions.

Know the Law

Laws regarding spousal inheritance vary greatly from state to state. The best way you can protect yourself from disinheritance is to familiarize yourself with the law in your state. If you can, consult an attorney who practices estate planning—not family law!—and learn the basics of what you are entitled to. You can also get information online, but I suggest consulting an attorney for two reasons: First, you can ask the attorney specific questions about your situation and get answers that address your particular concerns. Second, information online can be incorrect unless you get it from a reputable source, such as the local bar association web page. An estate planning attorney will know the law and give you correct answers; the attorney might even give you a free consultation. Here are some basic questions to ask:

- What does the state's elective share law guarantee you if you are left out of your spouse's will or receive a very small amount?
- Does the amount of the elective share change if you have children? Does it matter if the children are the joint children of you and your spouse or the children of one of you from a prior marriage?
- What property is included in the elective share? Does the "pot" from which your share is taken include the property in a living trust or other nonprobate property, such as joint tenancies and jointly held bank accounts?
- Does your state take into account the length of your marriage when determining elective share?
- Does your state count as part of your elective share your separate property—and subtract it from the amount of the share you get from your spouse's estate?
- What are you entitled to if your spouse dies without a will?

Become Actively Involved in Estate Planning

Everyone should have an estate plan—and married couples should have one they plan together with the help of an attorney. When you both meet the attorney, you become his or her "joint clients," which means the attorney cannot keep information from either of you that is relevant to your estate plan. So, for example, if your spouse wants to tell your attorney something in confidence that might affect your estate planning, the attorney will probably have to tell you, insist that your spouse tell you, or withdraw from representing you both. An ethical attorney will make sure you read and sign a letter stating that you understand this.

Doing your estate planning jointly offers two benefits. The first is that during the estate planning process, each person puts all their assets on the table, so to speak. One of the first steps your attorney will ask you to do is to draw up a list of your joint and separate assets. If one of you has separate property, this is a good opportunity to make sure you both know what it is.

A second is that it gives you a chance to discuss as a couple what your goals are. For example, most couples in first marriages want to leave everything to each other. But couples in second marriages with children from prior relationships often want to provide for those children as well. This might be a source of conflict. Discussing it with an attorney may make the conversation easier because your attorney will have dealt with this issue before and will probably have suggestions for how to provide for both the surviving spouse and the children in a fair and balanced way.

If your spouse isn't willing to engage in joint estate planning or is secretive about his assets, you can't force him to go through the estate planning process with you or share information about his assets. But that behavior is a red flag. Consult with an attorney about your rights and ask for suggestions for ways to proceed.

Ensure Beneficiary Designations Are Up to Date

As I explained earlier in the chapter, many financial instruments such as investment accounts, joint bank accounts, and life insurance policies are nonprobate property, meaning after your death they will not go through probate but pass on to whomever they designate as a beneficiary. In some states, these forms of property are not counted for purposes of calculating your share of the estate. So make sure you and your spouse have updated the beneficiary designations in all these accounts—and make sure you are a beneficiary on his accounts and vice versa!

If you are in a second marriage, confirm with your spouse that he has changed the beneficiary designation in all such plan documents to benefit you and not his ex-spouse—surely that's what your spouse wants too, but perhaps he has put it off or forgotten about it. Although state laws that revoke bequests to an ex-spouse usually apply to these financial instruments, it's much better to make sure the documents themselves are changed in the first place. Doing so avoids confusion and potentially litigation, and it saves time and money. Each instrument has its own rules for how to make the change correctly, so make sure those are followed—just making the change informally, like writing a note on the policy or writing it into a will, won't work.

Talk to Your Spouse about His ERISA-Governed Retirement Accounts

You can't do a lot about the inequities in ERISA-governed accounts that I discussed earlier. But if you know about them, you can plan for them. For example, if your husband has a retirement plan that is subject to ERISA, you now know that the lump-sum payment he gets on retirement will be paid to him alone and that he can dispose of it as he wishes. Why not have a conversation with him about it—now, before it's paid out—and talk about ways to invest it that would benefit both of you.

Be aware that if you want to leave part of your share of pension benefits in your will to someone but you die before your ERISA plan spouse, that may not work. (Remember Dorothy's story?) If you can, you're better off giving that person gifts while you are alive.

Finally, ERISA plans must provide benefits to surviving spouses. This means that if your husband dies before or after retirement, you might be entitled to a portion or all of the proceeds from that retirement account or what's called a "survivor's benefit." It's critical that you don't waive your survivor benefits. The only way to do this is in writing, with a special form that the ERISA plan administrator provides. So don't do this, and beware of anyone who asks you to!

CONCLUSION

In this chapter, I've shown you how the laws of inheritance—like the other areas of law I've been discussing—often cheat women. Particularly for women in second or third marriages, in which the husband has children from prior relationships, pitfalls abound. If this is you, there's good news: once you know the ways the law can cheat you, there's actually a lot you can do to outsmart it. Don't wait. Take action now!

The message of this book is simple: knowledge is power. Once you get past the misconception that the law treats women equally, and understand how it doesn't, you can protect yourself against its pitfalls.

But how could things be different? Can we imagine a legal system that did a better job of protecting women by taking account of the different ways they are situated with respect to careers, children, caretaking, retirement, and longevity? Actually, we don't have to look far: many European countries have laws that do offer women more protection than American laws do. And some states in the United States are developing and interpreting laws in ways that take account of women's often unequal situations and are helping them hold onto their wealth. So let's look at some of the bright spots.

Cohabitation

Remember how hard it was to get a fair division of property or earnings if you lived with someone without getting married—but contributed equally to the household and shared enterprise of the relationship?

How do other countries deal with the phenomenon of cohabitation? It's even more common in many European countries than it is in the United States; Americans have a much higher marriage rate than many European countries—France, for example. So how do they address property division when these relationships end?

The United Kingdom, for one, is working toward a solution to that problem right now: in July 2017, a Cohabitants Rights Bill was introduced in the House of Lords (basically the British Senate but also the Supreme Court).[21] This bill seeks to give financial protection to people who live together—especially the financially dependent partner. It would allow a court to issue something called a "financial settlement order" if one party gained a benefit from the other party's financial or other contributions or sacrifices during the relationship. The court can order a lump-sum payment, property division, or even pension sharing, based on the financial needs of the parties.

These are all remedies available to married couples in both the United States and the UK. But remember how hard it was for a woman who had chosen to keep house and support a man's career to get any kind of financial compensation when the relationship broke up if they weren't married? The outcome really depends, in the United States, on the state you live in—and even maybe the judge who hears your case. With this bill, the UK will offer a uniform national solution for someone in this situation, and it is a solution that recognizes one partner's needs and nonfinancial contributions.

France has what may be the most inclusive cohabitation rights of all. It allows almost any two people to register for a "civil solidarity pact."[22] The law was originally passed to give same-sex couples marital rights, but now many opposite-sex couples have embraced it as well as a way of formalizing a commitment without religious overtones—a popular option in secular France. The law allows any couple to register and entitles the partners to the same rights as married couples, such as income tax benefits, inheritance rights, and housing. The law covers virtually any two people sharing a home—it doesn't even imply or require a sexual relationship. It could apply to siblings or an elderly person and her caregiver, for example.

Imagine if this were available for the women caregivers I've discussed who lost out when the people they cared for didn't come through on their promises to leave them property—such as Hildegard in chapter 5 or Eleanor in chapter 1. If they had been registered for civil partnerships, they would have had a much better chance of seeing those promises kept and being compensated for their sacrifices. True, either party can end the partnership, but it must be done formally, and the other person must receive three months' notice before the dissolution is valid. In Hildegard's case, she would at least have had notice about her husband's change in plans and could have confronted him, but do you think he would have done it if he'd known she'd find out before his death? And in Eleanor's case, it seems likely that Walter simply forgot his promises to her when he wrote his will; registering for a partnership would have ensured her inheritance.

In 2005, New Zealand passed a law that granted property rights to people living in committed "marriage-like" relationships.[23] Under this statute, a cohabitant may bring a claim if the relationship lasted three years (although even if it lasted less than that, she may bring a claim if there was a child born from the relationship or if the court decides it must divide the property in order to prevent severe injustice). A court looks at all of the couple's property and divides it into "relationship" property and separate property, then divides the "relationship" property. New Zealand passed the law because its legislature recognized that the breakup of co-habitation relationships could often lead to injustice to the economically dependent partner, often the female partner if an opposite-sex relationship.

Premarital Agreements—Prenups

An important difference between American and European prenups is that the law of most European countries requires that a notary be present at the signing of any such agreement.[24] That may not sound like a big deal, because in the United States notaries are people who mostly look at your ID to see if you are who you say you are and then put their stamp on the agreement. But in Europe notaries are quite different: they are actually trained in the law, provide many types of legal services, and are required to offer legal advice to both parties signing an agreement. Thus, a European notary would be responsible for making sure that each person understood the agreement and what rights they might be giving up by signing it and that each party was signing knowingly and voluntarily. If the notary did not feel confident that these requirements were met, he or she could not legally validate the agreement. The purpose of the notary's role in overseeing prenups—or any other contract between private individuals—is to protect the weaker and less sophisticated party.[25]

Can you imagine what a difference it might make if a European-type of notary had to be present and sign off on prenups in the United States? Think back to the pregnancy cases, in which the woman had quit her job, moved to another state, and had no other place to live or means of support, and no health insurance. Do you think a notary standing in front of someone in that situation would sign off on the agreement that it was voluntary? In Europe, it would be the notary's responsibility to educate her about what she was giving up by signing and about what her alternatives were. It seems unlikely that an enforceable agreement would emerge from such a situation.

Even England, whose law is often closer to that of the United States, didn't enforce prenups until 2010.[26] Then, their Supreme Court decided to recognize the validity of such agreements, but with considerably more oversight than many American courts use; for example, UK courts must take into account the "emotional dynamics" at the execution of the agreement.[27] An examination of the emotional dynamics would probably have made a difference in the case of Mary, who claimed her doctor-fiancé insisted she get pregnant before he would marry her, and then when she did, insisted she sign a prenup. Remember how everyone involved agreed that she was crying when they met to discuss the agreement? Do you think scrutiny of the "emotional dynamics" of the execution would have led anyone to believe that she signed voluntarily? Or what about all the other cases of the "pregnant brides"? Or what about the women who saw the prenup for the first time a few days before the wedding? A review of the emotional dynamics of these situations seems as if it would have changed the outcomes, don't you think? But American courts, although they sometimes do find these contracts void for issues like fairness or duress, generally ignore these dynamics. It makes a big difference for women.

In general, the UK decision that allowed for the enforcement of prenups required courts to look at the fairness of the contract. As we've seen, while some American courts do this, many do not—all they are interested in is the "voluntariness" of the signing, and the standards they use in judging this "voluntariness" are very limited. Would a court truly examining the fairness of the Joseph and Susan's prenup in chapter 2 have concluded that it was fair when Joseph walked away with his $100-plus million, leaving Susan, after a ten-year marriage and two children with basically a house and a car?

And there are American courts that have treated prenups fairly and with an understanding of what might constitute duress for a woman faced with the demand to sign one. For example, Erin's fiancé, John, handed her the prenup for the first time forty-eight hours before their wedding.[28] When they had first met, six years earlier, John was fifty-two and Erin was twenty-two. He was a successful real estate investor with assets of about six million dollars, while Erin had about five thousand dollars' worth of personal property and had dropped out of high school in the eleventh grade and only worked low-level jobs. In fact, when they started dating, John encouraged Erin to stop working and to let him support her.

Unbeknownst to Erin, John owed his ex-wife several million dollars from their divorce settlement. Maybe that's why he wanted a prenup, but whatever the reason, he left an article about prenups out on the kitchen counter one day after they had become engaged. (Can you say "passive aggressive"?) When Erin found it, she—to her credit—got furious and told John she'd never sign such an agreement.

John let it drop, but again, unbeknownst to Erin (is there a pattern here?), contacted his lawyers and asked them to draw up a prenup. Erin first heard about it two days before the wedding. John's lawyer hired a recent law school graduate in the same firm to represent Erin, and they met to go over it the day before the wedding—the first time Erin saw it. Erin's lawyer actually did the best for her he could under the circumstances: he negotiated a better deal than the original draft, leaving her with one-sixth of John's estate in the event of divorce or death. But he also advised Erin not sign it and told her that John's disclosure of assets had been inadequate; he even assured her that she could postpone the wedding.

But the wedding was the next day. The two hundred guests had already arrived. Erin's parents had flown in from Thailand. Everything had been paid for. She signed the prenup. Throughout the process, she was crying and so distressed that at times she was unable to speak.

So far this sounds a lot like cases I told you about in the chapter on prenups, doesn't it? So you may think you can predict how it came out. John died ten years later, and Erin challenged the prenup, saying she had signed it under duress. The trial court ruled against her, and she appealed. The appeals court found that there had indeed been duress.

First, it said that Erin should have been able to trust her fiancé to treat her with honesty and fairness, and that he had failed to do so. (Remember Susan, who the court said should have expected her fiancé to lie to her and wouldn't get her out of the prenup just because he had? See how different courts can be?)

Next, the court agreed that Erin had been under duress because of the timing of the signing right before the wedding and because she had had no time to verify John's statements about his assets. It recognized that if she had called off the wedding, she would have had no place to live and no means of support. Because of all these factors, the court invalidated the prenup, and Erin was able to inherit.

(Of course, notice that the first wife—remember the one John owed millions to because of the divorce decree?—was the one who got left out in the cold this time. What's the lesson here? Longevity bites. Because of John's sneaky ways, one of the women surviving him was going to get cheated. It was really only a question of which one.)

This case is really a lesson in how court's decisions vary dramatically from state to state (they sometimes even vary from court to court within a state). Remember Mary Anne from chapter 2—who had left her job, moved, and was seven months' pregnant when she signed? If the court in the above case found duress where Erin was dependent on John and afraid of embarrassment and losing her only means of support, what do you think it would have found in Mary Anne's case? And what about the case of Gita, who was bipolar? What about Victoria, who signed a prenup that didn't even list the value of her fiancé's assets?

As I've said before, the cases I discussed in the earlier chapters are the worst scenarios. Similar cases have come out more fairly in other courts, as I'm showing in this chapter. But the thing is, it's hard to predict how your case will come out. Maybe you're in a state with a history of fair rulings in prenup cases, but maybe you're not. That's why I'm saying, don't count on courts to protect you. That's why I've given you ways to protect yourself. I hope you use them.

Divorce

In the case of *White v. White*, English courts adopted the standard of equality—not equity—for property division upon divorce. You may remember my explaining in the chapter on divorce that most American courts use a yardstick of equity—that is, fairness—in dividing property and that this doesn't mean equality. I also discussed the ways courts fail to give women credit for their domestic and unpaid labor that helps their husband's careers and businesses.

Concerned about these very issues, English courts have explicitly adopted an equality standard for property division, beginning with *White v. White*.

Mr. and Mrs. White ran a very successful dairy farming partnership and a separate farm together, which over the years generated 4.5 million pounds in assets (about 6 million dollars). When they divorced, the trial judge awarded Mrs. White a fifth of the assets, explaining that it would be a shame to break up the existing business just to give Mrs. White more. The appeals court increased her share to two-fifths, noting that she had been an equal partner in the business. (You're following this, right? Because I'm not!)

She appealed again. This time, the House of Lords—the British Supreme Court—declared that the property should be divided equally between the spouses. This decision changed the course of English divorce law. This was 1997. From then on, the presumption in divorce cases in England is that the court will divide the property equally—not just equitably!—between the spouses.

And there are bright spots here in the United States as well. As far back as 1979, a Delaware court ordered a divorcing couple to perform an annual "equalization" of their spendable incomes. When Ruth and Adam were married, she worked as an airline attendant. At about the same time she became engaged, the airline offered her a management position that she turned down at the request of her fiancé. She left her job, moved with her now husband to Wilmington, Delaware, where he worked as a manager in a chemical company. During the twenty-year marriage, she stayed home and raised the couple's children, took care of the house, and supported her husband's career. The husband did well, received promotions and annual raises of about 10 percent. After twenty years, the husband filed for divorce.

The court did something unprecedented. It ordered that the property be divided as equally as possible and that their future spendable—that is, discretionary—income should be equalized between them. The court made this decision based on its finding that the marriage was a true partnership "in every sense of the word." The husband appealed—and the appeals court affirmed the ruling. Nice change, isn't it?

Notice that as early as 1979, a court was able to understand that a non-wage-earning spouse's contributions to the marital partnership were worth as much as those of the wage-earning spouse. This case still influences alimony decisions to this day. If you've been a stay-at-home mom who gave up career opportunities and are getting divorced in Delaware, you may get justice. This may be because Delaware courts are known to specialize in corporate and partnership law: maybe they know a "true partnership" when they see it and have an understanding for what "sweat equity" means.

Caregiving

Hildegard and Eleanor would have really benefited from the availability of something like the French solidary pact, wouldn't they? If such a thing were available here, they would have had a valid legal documents to enforce their right to compensation—and no one prying into their sex lives either. This gender-neutral, sex-neutral—relationship neutral—contract is a way to make sure you make up for some of the sacrifices you make when caring for loved ones.

Domestic Violence

Some states in the United States now have laws that make it illegal for employers to fire workers because they are domestic violence victims, even if that domestic violence comes to work. Other countries have addressed this issue on a national level: South Africa, for example, passed a law in 1998 called the Domestic Violence Act, which, among other things, makes it illegal to fire someone for gender-based reasons, and it includes gender-based violence as one of those reasons. Under this law, Philloria and Kim could have kept their jobs and their financial independence, giving them a much better chance of getting and staying away from their abusers.

Spousal Inheritance

Many European countries have the same system of community property we have in nine states—not surprising since those states got it from the European countries that have it! This is the case of France and the Netherlands and several other countries. Speaking broadly, it's similar to community property regimes in the United States' community property states: the property earned by either spouse during the marriage is marital property and each spouse has a 50 percent interest in it.

Some countries, however, offer additional protections for the surviving spouse. For example, in France, it's almost impossible to disinherit your spouse by putting assets into a domestic trust, as we saw here, because French law limits what you can use a trust for. In fact, under French law, you can't create a trust for an individual private beneficiary. So, if you remember the case of Kathleen, whose husband put most of his estate into a trust for his daughter and left much less to his wife, you can see how French trust law would have made that impossible. I'm not saying it's impossible to disinherit your spouse in France, but at least this avenue is closed off, and it's a lot harder.

Here in the United States, some states also make it much harder than others to disinherit your spouse. You'll recall that all the states guarantee a surviving spouse a share of her husband's estate but that the devil was in the details: What was included in the "estate" in the first place? How big was the "pot" she took her share from? And how easy was it for the husband to shrink it before he died?

States such as Delaware require that the estate include pretty much every form of property the husband had control over when he died (they took their cue from the Internal Revenue Code, which is very good at taxing as much as possible). He set up a trust but still had access to the funds? Into the pot. Owned property jointly with someone other than the surviving spouse? Into the pot. Gave away large chunks of your estate to other people so your surviving spouse wouldn't get it? If he did it within two years of death—back into the pot (because he gave the property away within two years of death, it's assumed that he did it in order to cheat the surviving spouse out of it when he died; that's the rationale for putting it back in). Set up a joint bank account with someone other than you? Pot. Put someone besides you as the beneficiary on a stock account? Pot, pot, pot.

It gets better—I mean, fairer and fairer. Maybe he tried to outsmart the law by setting up an irrevocable trust but kept getting the income for life. Nice try, but guess what? All the assets in the trust are considered part of his estate.

In states that follow this approach, it's much harder to disinherit the surviving spouse. Take the case of Anna, who was married to Clarence for thirty years. About twenty years in, Clarence decided to set up a trust with him and his son as cotrustees. Throughout the rest of his life, Clarence got distributions on a regular basis from the trust, he managed its investment, and he kept the right to terminate it at any time he wanted. Then he executed a will leaving most of his estate to the trust. He left Anna some household items and $10,000.

Anna, unsurprisingly, decided to reject her bequest under the will and exercise her right under state law to take her share of

Clarence's estate, and she said the trust should be counted as part of the estate. The son, who now stood to get distributions from the trust and the new beneficiary, disagreed. They went to court. The court said that the trust had to be counted as part of the estate for the purpose of calculating Anna's share because Clarence hadn't really given away the property. He had kept so much control and benefit over it—getting payments and keeping the right to terminate it and to withdraw as much money as he wanted at any time—that for all intents and purposes it had still been his property at his death. The court said it would be unfair to Anna, the surviving spouse, to treat it as anything but part of the estate. So the pot from which Anna would take her share just got a lot bigger—actually reflecting what Clarence really owned at his death.

Remember the case of Kathleen, who argued that her husband's revocable trust should be counted as part of his estate? Pretty similar set of facts, wouldn't you say? In that case, as you may recall, the court ruled against Kathleen, saying that the trust did not have to count as part of the husband's estate for purposes of her share. Why the different outcomes? Different states. Remember what I keep saying: the state—even the court—you live in can make all the difference. Plan for the worst and hope for the best.

Some states have also seen through the life insurance trick as well. Remember that one way a spouse could shrink his estate was by spending money on a lavish life insurance policy and then naming someone besides his wife as beneficiary? Well, some states have put an end to that.

For example, take Nimia, whose husband, José, died and left her about $4,000 worth of personal property. The only other asset he had was a life insurance policy worth $30,000, but he had listed someone else as the beneficiary. Nimia argued that the proceeds of the insurance policy should be counted as part of the pot from which she took her share, and the court agreed.

Final Thoughts

So my message is twofold. First, there are bright spots on the horizon: many American courts and foreign countries are pioneering new ways to ensure that the law stops robbing women of wealth. Your fate as a fiancée, separated cohabitant, divorced spouse, caregiver, surviving spouse, or victim of domestic violence may depend largely on what state you live in when you need the law to protect you and your wealth. And truth be told, there are still many jurisdictions that do not protect you from the law's robbery.

But my other message is this: there's a lot you can do to protect yourself. As this book has shown, even in states that are behind the curve with respect to protecting women's wealth, you can use your understanding of the law's inadequacies to your advantage. Cohabiting in a state that won't recognize your claim to part of the wealth you helped create? Being pressured to sign a prenup you think might be unfair? Already signed one and are now regretting it? Facing divorce as a spouse who cut back on career and education to support your spouse? A victim of financial abuse by your partner? Want to find a way to care for a loved one without condemning yourself to poverty in old age? Want to protect your inheritance as a surviving spouse? Now you know what to do: look up the law in your state (it's easy to do now that you know the issues). Stick your nose into family finances if it isn't already there. Consult a lawyer if you need to. And draft a contract!

NOTES

1. THE LEGAL PITFALLS
OF LIVING TOGETHER

1. *Costa v. Oliven*, 849 N.E.2d 122 (Ill. App. 2006). I have reversed the genders of the plaintiff and defendant to reflect the more common facts of this kind of case.

2. Makini Brice, "Reasons Why a Third of Babies in U.S. Are Unintended: Cohabitation and Contraception," *Medical Daily*, July 25, 2012, www.medicaldaily.com.

3. Rachael Rettner, "More Couples Living Together outside of Marriage," LiveScience, April 4, 2013, https://www.livescience.com.

4. "Divorce," LoveToKnow, https://divorce.lovetoknow.com.

5. Colorado, District of Columbia, Iowa, Kansas, Montana, New Hampshire, Oklahoma, Rhode Island, Texas, and Utah.

6. Heidi Glenn, "No, You're Not in a Common-Law Marriage after 7 Years Together," NPR, September 4, 2016, https://www.npr.org.

7. See *Maria v. Freitas*, 832 P.2d 259 (Haw. 1992); *Bright v. Kuehl*, 650 N.E.2d 311 (Ind. Ct. App. 1995); *Kerkove v. Thompson*, 487 N.W.2d 693 (Iowa Ct. App. 1992); *Ellis v. Berry*, 867 P.2d 1063 (Kan. Ct. App. 1993); *Connel v. Francisco*, 898 P.2d 831 (Wash. 1995).

8. *Connel v. Francisco*, 898 P.2d 831 (Wash. 1995).

9. See Minn. Stat. Ann. § 513.075 (West 1990); *Tarry v. Stewart*, 649 N.E.2d 1 (Ohio 1994).

10. *Gazvoda v. Wright*, 878 N.E.2d 219 (App. Crt. Ind. 2007).

11. *Lorch v. Lorch*, 2005 WL 3455879 (Cal. App.).

12. *Nichols v. Funderburk*, 881 So.2d 266 (Miss. App. 2003).

13. "Quantum Meruit Law and Legal Definition," US Legal, accessed August 16, 2019, https://definitions.uslegal.com.

14. *Snell v. Meyers*, 2001 WL 732082 (2001).

15. *Darling v. Crow*, 2015 WL 2383835 (Vt.).

16. *Tarry v. Stewart*, 649 N.E.2d 1 (N.D. 1994).

17. *Adkins v. Estate of Walter William Washut*, 892 P.2d 128 (1995).

18. *Adkins v. Estate of Walter William Washut*, 892 P.2d 128 (1995).

19. *Adkins v. Estate of Walter William Washut*, 892 P.2d 128 (1995).

20. *Murphy v. Bitsoih*, 320 F. Supp. 1174 (2004).

21. RCW 26.60.010.

2. THE TRUTH ABOUT
PRENUPTIAL AGREEMENTS

1. *Porreco v. Porreco*, 811 A.2d 566, 570 (Pa. 2002).

2. *Teed v. Teed*, 2013 WL 2149857.

3. *Biliouris v. Biliouris*, 852 N.E.2d 687, 693 (Mass. App. Ct. 2006).

4. *Williams v. Walker Thomas Furniture*, 350 F.2d 445 (D.C. Cir. 1965).

5. *Austin Inst. Inc. v. Loral Corp*, 272 N.E.2d 533 (1971).

6. *Mallen v. Mallen*, 622 S.E.2d 812 (2005).

7. *Hardee v. Hardee*, 585 S.E.2d 501 (2003).

8. *Finkelstein v. Finkelstein*, WL 2012 WL 1252680 (N.Y. App. 2012).

9. *Estate of Menahem*, 847 N.Y.S.2d 903 (2007).

10. *Wilkes v. Estate of Wilkes*, 33527 P.3d 433 (Mt. 2001).

11. *Friezo v. Friezo*, 914 A.2d 533 (2007).

12. *Dematteo v. Dematteo*, 762 N.E.2d 797 (Mass. 2002).

3. HOW DIVORCE LEAVES WOMEN
OUT IN THE COLD

1. Amelia Hill, "Men Become Richer after Divorce," *Guardian*, January 24, 2009, https://www.theguardian.com.

2. Sharon Johnson, "Hidden Divorce Penalty Is Older Age Poverty," Women's eNews, September 3, 2015, https://womensenews.org.

3. National Center on Caregiving, "Women and Caregiving: Facts and Figures," Family Caregiver Alliance, December 31, 2003, https:// www.caregiver.org.

4. www.library.pcw.gov.ph/.../ wives%20relative%20wages,%20husbands%20paid%20work.p.

5. Ibid.

6. Chloe Tejada, "Women Still Do More Chores at Home than Men, Study Finds," *HuffPost*, September 27, 2017, https://www.huffington post.ca.

7. National Alliance for Caregiving, "The MetLife Study of Caregiving Costs to Working Caregivers," June 2011, https://www.caregiving.org.

8. LawFirms, "Alimony," accessed August 16, 2019, https://www .lawfirms.com.

9. Ibid.

10. Ibid.

11. Alabama, Arkansas, Delaware, Illinois, Louisiana, North Carolina, North Dakota, Pennsylvania, South Carolina, Texas, and Utah.

12. *Keller v. O'Brien*, 652 N.E.2d 589 (Mass. 1995).

13. *In re Marriage of Susan*, 367 Ill. App. 3d 926 (2006).

14. See Mo. Rev. Stat. § 452.370(1) (2016).

15. *Murphy v. Murphy*, 201 So.2d 18 (2013).

16. *Rester v. Rester*, 5 So.3d 1132 (2008).

17. *In re Marriage of Herrin*, 634 N.E.2d 199 (Ill. App. 1994).

18. Laura Barnett, "Why Do So Many Women Cede Control of Family Finances?" *Guardian*, May 28, 2012, https://www.theguardian.com.

19. *Kuder v. Schroeder*, 430 S.E.2d 271 (N.C. 1993).

20. *Wendt v. Wendt*, 757 A.2d 1225 (Conn. App. Ct. 2000).

21. Betsy Morris, "It's Her Job Too: Lorna Wendt's $20 Million Divorce Case Is the Shot Heard 'round the Water Cooler," *Fortune*, February 2, 1998, http://money.cnn.com.

22. Victoria McKee, "Marrying the Company," *Times* (London), July 11, 1988.

23. Sharon Walsh, "For Corporate Spouses, an Unlimited Partnership," *Washington Post*, January 4, 1998.

24. Ibid.

25. McKee, "Marrying the Company."

26. See Bonnie Miller Rubin and Jon Anderson, "What Is an Exec's Wife Worth? Plenty, If You Ask the Court," *Chicago Tribune*, December 14, 1997.

27. Ibid.

28. Walsh, "For Corporate Spouses."

29. *Becker v. Perkins-Becker*, 669 A.2d 524 (R.I. 1996).

30. Cited in Penelope Eileen Bryan, "Women's Freedom to Contract at Divorce: A Mask for Contextual Coercion," *Buffalo Law Review* 47, no. 3 (1999): 1153–274.

4. THE ROLE OF THE LAW
IN PERPETUATING DOMESTIC ABUSE

1. Michael S. Kimmel, "Male Victims of Domestic Violence: A Substantive and Methodology Research Review," VAWnet, January 2001, https://vawnet.org.

2. Corporate Alliance to End Partner Violence, "Domestic Violence Exerts Significant Impact on America's Workplaces, Benchmark Study Finds," PR Newswire, October 12, 2005, http://www.caepv.org.

3. U.S. General Accounting Office, *Domestic Violence: Prevalence and Implications for Employment among Welfare Recipients* (Washington, DC: Author, 1998), 7–9, 18–19; see also National Employment Law Project (NELP), *Unemployment Insurance for Survivors of Domestic Violence* (New York: Author, 2003), 1.

4. Ibid.

5. Ibid.

6. Ibid.

7. Ibid.

8. Ibid.

9. *Green v. Bryant*, 887 F.Supp. 798 (Pa. 1995).

10. Robin R. Runge and Marcellene E. Hearn, "Employment Rights Advocacy for Domestic Violence Victims," *Domestic Violence Report* 5, no. 2 (December/January 2000): 17–18, 26–29. Reprinted in Nancy K. D. Lemon, *Domestic Violence Law* (Eagan, MN: West Group, 2001), 821–22.

11. National Center for Injury Prevention and Control, Department of Health and Human Services, "Costs of Intimate Partner Violence against Women in the United States," February 18, 2003, http://www.cdc.gov.

12. Health, Education, and Human Services Division, U.S. General Accounting Office, "Domestic Violence: Prevalence and Implications for Employment among Welfare Recipients," November 1998, http://www.gao.gov, 19.

13. If you are in this situation, it's important that you know the law in your state: you can find out what kinds of legal protections are available to you as an employee by looking up the following resource on Legal Momentum: "Know Your Rights: Time Off to Participate in Criminal Proceedings," 2005. http://www.legalmomentum.org. In addition, federal employees are granted paid leave to serve as a witness in a case in which the government is a party: 5 U.S.C. §§ 5515, 5537, 6322 (2000).

14. *O'Brien v. O'Brien*, 489 N.E.2d 712, 719 (1985).

15. *In re Marriage of Coomer*, 622 N.E.2d 1315 (Ind. Ct. App. 1993).

16. *Twyman v. Twyman*, 855 S.W.2d 619, 620 (Tex. 1993).

17. *Cusseaux v. Pickett*, 652 A.2d 789 (N.J. Sup. Ct. Law Div. 1995).

18. Sarah M. Buel, "Access to Meaningful Remedy: Overcoming Doctrinal Obstacles in Tort Litigation against Domestic Violence Offenders," *Oregon Law Review* 83 (2004): 945–1034.

19. *O'Keiff v. Christ*, No. 92–28795-A (Dist. Ct. Tex., Apr. 6, 1994).

20. Carolyn Magnuson, "Marital Tort Lawsuits Can Make Abusers Pay," *Trial* 38, no. 2 (February 2002): 12–13.

5. CAREGIVING'S COST TO WOMEN

1. *Borelli v. Brousseau*, 12 Cal. App. 4th 647 (1993).

2. Annalyn Kurtz, "Why 26% of U.S. Women Still Choose Not to Work," CNN Business, August 13, 2013, http://money.cnn.com.

3. National Center on Caregiving, "Women and Caregiving: Facts and Figures," Family Caregiver Alliance, December 31, 2003, https://www.caregiver.org.

4. Ibid.

5. Ibid.

6. Ibid.

7. Ibid.

8. John Schall, "Caregiving Is Forcing Women 50+ to Leave the Workforce," *Forbes*, October 10, 2016, https://www.forbes.com.

9. National Alliance for Caregiving, "The MetLife Study of Caregiving Costs to Working Caregivers," June 2011, https://www.caregiving.org.

10. Ibid.

11. Ibid.

12. Ibid.

13. Ibid.

14. *Cragle v. Gray*, 206 P.3d 446 (2009).

15. WorkLife Law, "Frequently Asked Questions about Family Responsibilities Discrimination," accessed August 16, 2019, http://worklifelaw.org.

6. DISINHERITED—THE FATE
OF THE SURVIVING SPOUSE

1. *Karsenty v. Shoukroun*, 945 A.2d 1270 (2008).

2. Jeffrey M. Jones, "Majority in U.S. Do Not Have a Will," Gallup, May 18, 2016, https://news.gallup.com.

3. A. W. B. Simpson, *A History of the Land Law*, 2nd ed. (Oxford: Oxford University Press, 1986), 68–70.

4. Mark E. Williams, "Why Do Women Live Longer than Men? What Factors Explain Female Longevity?" *Psychology Today*, February 4, 2017, https://www.psychologytoday.com.

5. *Dumas v. Estate of Dumas*, 627 N.E.2d 978 (Ohio 1994).

6. *Friedberg v. Sunbank/Miami, N.A.*, 648 So.2d 204 (Fla. 1994).

7. *Nancy Powell-Ferri v. John Ferri*, SJC 12070 (2016).

8. *Bongaards v. Millen*, 793 N.E.2d 335 (2003). I have changed the facts of this case slightly to reflect the statistically more likely possibility

that the wife will be the disinherited spouse; in this case, it was the husband.

9. *Estate of Myers*, 825 N.W.2d 1 (2012).

10. *Traub v. Zlatkiss*, 559 So.2d 445 (1990).

11. *Estate of Francis*, 394 S.E.2d 150 (N.C. 1990).

12. See Conn. Gen. Stat. Ann. § 45a-436 (West 2004) (providing for a one-third life estate in the probate estate); R.I. Gen. Laws § 33-25-2 (2008) (providing for a life estate in all of the decedent's real property).

13. Ashlea Ebeling, "IRS Announces 2017 Estate and Gift Tax Limits: The $11 Million Tax Break," *Forbes*, October 25, 2016, https://www.forbes.com.

14. *Estate of Clack v. Commissioner*, 106 T.C. 131, 132 (1996).

15. Wendy C. Gerzog, "The Marital Deduction QTIP Provisions: Illogical and Degrading to Women," *UCLA Women's Law Journal* 5, no. 2 (1995): 301–27.

16. *Boggs v. Boggs*, 520 U.S. 833 (1997).

17. Lois Shaw and Catherine Hill, *The Gender Gap in Pension Coverage: What Does the Future Hold?* IWPR Publication E507 (Washington, DC: Institute for Women's Policy Research, 2002).

18. *United States v. Craft*, 535 U.S. 274 (2002).

19. *Estate of Alberts*, 875 N.W.2d 427 (Neb. 2016).

20. Mary Ann Glendon, *The New Family and the New Property* (Toronto: Butterworth, 1981), 66.

21. Parliament.uk, "Cohabitation Rights Bill [HL] 2017-19," accessed August 16, 2019, https://services.parliament.uk.

22. Notaires de France, "Couple/Famille," accessed August 16, 2019, https://www.notaires.fr.

23. Te Tari Taiwhenua, Department of Internal Affairs, "Civil Union," accessed August 16, 2019, https://www.dia.govt.nz.

24. European Justice, "European Judicial Network: Netherlands," last updated October 23, 2018, https://e-justice.europa.eu.

25. National Notary Association, "Common Law versus Civil Law Notaries," *Notary Bulletin* (blog), November 28, 2011, https://www.natio nalnotary.org.

26. Owen Bowcott, "Prenup Agreement Enforced under UK Law," *Guardian*, October 20, 2010, https://www.theguardian.com.

27. *MacLeod v. MacLeod* ([2008] UKPC 64, [2010] 1 A.C. 298).

28. *Estate of Hollett*, 834 A.2d. 348 (N.H. 2003).

BIBLIOGRAPHY

CASES

Adkins v. Estate of Walter William Washut, 892 P.2d 128 (1995)
Austin Inst. Inc. v. Loral Corp, 272 N.E.2d 533 (1971)
Becker v. Perkins-Becker, 669 A.2d 524 (R.I. 1996)
Biliouris v. Biliouris, 852 N.E.2d 687, 693 (Mass. App. Ct. 2006)
Boggs v. Boggs, 520 U.S. 833 (1997)
Bongaards v. Millen, 793 N.E.2d. 335 (2003)
Borelli v. Brousseau, 12 Cal. App. 4th 647 (1993)
Bright v. Kuehl, 650 N.E.2d 311 (Ind. Ct. App. 1995)
Connel v. Francisco, 898 P.2d 831 (Wash. 1995)
Costa v. Oliven, 849 N.E.2d 122 (Ill. App. 2006)
Cragle v. Gray, 206 P.3d 446 (2009)
Cusseaux v. Pickett, 652 A.2d 789 (N.J. Sup. Ct. Law Div. 1995)
Darling v. Crow, 2015 WL 2383835 (Vt.)
Dematteo v. Dematteo, 762 N.E.2d 797 (Mass. 2002)
Dumas v. Estate of Dumas, 627 N.E.2d 978 (Ohio 1994)
Ellis v. Berry, 867 P.2d 1063 (Kan. Ct. App. 1993)
Estate of Alberts, 875 N.W.2d 427 (Neb. 2016)
Estate of Clack v. Commissioner, 106 T.C. 131, 132 (1996)
Estate of Francis, 394 S.E.2d 150 (N.C. 1990)
Estate of Hollett, 834 A.2d 348 (N.H. 2003)
Estate of Menahem, 847 N.Y.S.2d 903 (2007)
Estate of Myers, 825 N.W.2d 1 (2012)
Finkelstein v. Finkelstein, WL 2012 WL 1252680 (N.Y. App. 2012)
Friedberg v. Sunbank/Miami, N.A., 648 So.2d 204 (Fla. 1994)
Friezo v. Friezo, 914 A.2d 533 (2007)
Gazvoda v. Wright, 872 N.E.2d 219 (App. Crt Ind. 2007)
Green v. Bryant, 887 F.Supp. 798 (Pa. 1995)
Hardee v. Hardee, 585 S.E.2d 501 (2003)
Holterman v. Holterman, 814 N.E.2d 765 (N.Y. 2004)
In re Marriage of Coomer, 622 N.E.2d 1315 (Ind. Ct. App. 1993)

In re Marriage of Herrin, 634 N.E.2d 199 (Ill. App. 1994)
In re Marriage of Susan, 367 Ill. App. 3d 926 (2006)
Karsenty v. Shoukroun, 945 A.2d 1270 (2008)
Keller v. O'Brien, 652 N.E.2d 589 (Mass. 1995)
Kerkove v. Thompson, 487 N.W.2d 693 (Iowa Ct. App. 1992)
Kuder v. Schroeder, 430 S.E.2d 271 (N.C. 1993)
Lorch v. Lorch, 2005 WL 3455879 (Cal. App.)
MacLeod v. MacLeod ([2008] UKPC 64, [2010] 1 A.C. 298)
Mallen v. Mallen, 822 S.E.2d 812 (2005)
Maria v. Freitas, 832 P.2d 259 (Haw. 1992)
Murphy v. Bitsoih, 320 F. Supp. 1174 (2004)
Murphy v. Murphy, 201 So.2d 18 (2013)
Nancy Powell-Ferri v. John Ferri, SJC 12070 (2016)
Nichols v. Funderburk, 881 So.2d 266 (Miss. App. 2003)
O'Brien v. O'Brien, 489 N.E.2d 712, 719 (1985).
O'Keiff v. Christ, No. 92-28795-A (Dist. Ct. Tex., Apr. 6, 1994)
Porreco v. Porreco, 811 A.2d 566, 570 (Pa. 2002)
Rester v. Rester, 5 So.3d 1132 (2008)
Snell v. Meyers, 2001 WL 732082 (2001)
Tarry v. Stewart, 649 N.E.2d 1 (N.D. 1994)
Tarry v. Stewart, 649 N.E.2d 1 (Ohio 1994)
Teed v. Teed, 2013 WL 2149857
Traub v. Zlatkiss, 559 So.2d 445 (1990)
Twyman v. Twyman, 855 S.W.2d 619, 620 (Tex. 1993)
United States v. Craft, 535 U.S. 274 (2002)
Wendt v. Wendt, 757 A.2d 1225 (Conn. App. Ct. 2000)
Wilkes v. Estate of Wilkes, 33527 P.3d 433 (Mt. 2001)
Williams v. Walker Thomas Furniture, 350 F.2d 445 (D.C. Cir. 1965)

WEBSITES

Barnett, Laura. "Why Do So Many Women Cede Control of Family Finances?" *Guardian*, May 28, 2012. https://www.theguardian.com.
Bowcott, Owen. "Prenup Agreement Enforced under UK Law." *Guardian*, October 20, 2010. https://www.theguardian.com.
Brice, Makini. "Reasons Why a Third of Babies in U.S. Are Unintended: Cohabitation and Contraception." *Medical Daily*, July 25, 2012. www.medicaldaily.com.
Corporate Alliance to End Partner Violence. "Domestic Violence Exerts Significant Impact on America's Workplaces, Benchmark Study Finds." PR Newswire, October 12, 2005. http://www.caepv.org.
"Divorce." LoveToKnow. https://divorce.lovetoknow.com.
Ebeling, Ashlea. "IRS Announces 2017 Estate and Gift Tax Limits: The $11 Million Tax Break." *Forbes*, October 25, 2016. https://www.forbes.com.
European Justice. "European Judicial Network: Netherlands." Last updated October 23, 2018. https://e-justice.europa.eu.
Glenn, Heidi. "No, You're Not in a Common-Law Marriage after 7 Years Together." NPR, September 4, 2016. https://www.npr.org.
Health, Education, and Human Services Division, U.S. General Accounting Office. "Domestic Violence: Prevalence and Implications for Employment among Welfare Recipients." November 1998. http://www.gao.gov.

Hill, Amelia. "Men Become Richer after Divorce." *Guardian*, January 24, 2009. https://www.theguardian.com.

Johnson, Sharon. "Hidden Divorce Penalty Is Older Age Poverty." Women's eNews, September 3, 2015. https://womensenews.org.

Jones, Jeffrey M. "Majority in U.S. Do Not Have a Will." Gallup, May 18, 2016. https://news.gallup.com.

Kimmel, Michael S. "Male Victims of Domestic Violence: A Substantive and Methodology Research Review." VAWnet, January 2001. https://vawnet.org.

Kurtz, Annalyn. "Why 26% of U.S. Women Still Choose Not to Work." CNN Business, August 13, 2013. http://money.cnn.com.

LawFirms. "Alimony." Accessed August 16, 2019. https://www.lawfirms.com.

Legal Momentum. "Know Your Rights: Time Off to Participate in Criminal Proceedings." 2005. http://www.legalmomentum.org.

Morris, Betsy. "It's Her Job Too: Lorna Wendt's $20 Million Divorce Case Is the Shot Heard 'round the Water Cooler." *Fortune*, February 2, 1998. http://money.cnn.com.

National Alliance for Caregiving. "The MetLife Study of Caregiving Costs to Working Caregivers." June 2011. https://www.caregiving.org.

National Center for Injury Prevention and Control, Department of Health and Human Services. "Costs of Intimate Partner Violence against Women in the United States." February 18, 2003. http://www.cdc.gov.

National Center on Caregiving. "Women and Caregiving: Facts and Figures." Family Caregiver Alliance, December 31, 2003. https://www.caregiver.org.

National Notary Association. "Common Law versus Civil Law Notaries." *Notary Bulletin* (blog), November 28, 2011. https://www.nationalnotary.org.

Notaires de France. "Couple/Famille." Accessed August 16, 2019. https://www.notaires.fr.

Parliament.uk. "Cohabitation Rights Bill [HL] 2017–19." Accessed August 16, 2019. https://services.parliament.uk.

Rettner, Rachael. "More Couples Living Together outside of Marriage." LiveScience, April 4, 2013. https://www.livescience.com.

Schall, John. "Caregiving Is Forcing Women 50+ to Leave the Workforce." *Forbes*, October 10, 2016. https://www.forbes.com.

Tejada, Chloe. "Women Still Do More Chores at Home than Men, Study Finds." *HuffPost*, September 27, 2017. https://www.huffingtonpost.ca.

Te Tari Taiwhenua, Department of Internal Affairs. "Civil Union." Accessed August 16, 2019. https://www.dia.govt.nz.

US Legal. "Quantum Meruit Law and Legal Definition." Accessed August 16, 2019. https://definitions.uslegal.com.

Williams, Mark E. "Why Do Women Live Longer than Men? What Factors Explain Female Longevity?" *Psychology Today*, February 4, 2017. https://www.psychologytoday.com.

WorkLife Law. "Frequently Asked Questions about Family Responsibilities Discrimination." Accessed August 16, 2019. http://worklifelaw.org.

BOOKS AND ARTICLES

Bryan, Penelope Eileen. "Women's Freedom to Contract at Divorce: A Mask for Contextual Coercion." *Buffalo Law Review* 47, no. 3 (1999): 1153–274.

Buel, Sarah M. "Access to Meaningful Remedy: Overcoming Doctrinal Obstacles in Tort Litigation against Domestic Violence Offenders." *Oregon Law Review* 83 (2004): 945–1034.

Gerzog, Wendy C. "The Marital Deduction QTIP Provisions: Illogical and Degrading to Women." *UCLA Women's Law Journal* 5, no. 2 (1995): 301–27.

Glendon, Mary Ann. *The New Family and the New Property*. Toronto: Butterworth, 1981.

Magnuson, Carolyn. "Marital Tort Lawsuits Can Make Abusers Pay." *Trial* 38, no. 2 (February 2002): 12–13.

McKee, Victoria. "Marrying the Company." *Times* (London), July 11, 1988.

Miller Rubin, Bonnie and Jon Anderson. "What Is an Exec's Wife Worth? Plenty, If You Ask the Court." *Chicago Tribune*, December 14, 1997.

National Employment Law Project (NELP). *Unemployment Insurance for Survivors of Domestic Violence*. New York: Author, 2003.

Runge, Robin R., and Marcellene E. Hearn. "Employment Rights Advocacy for Domestic Violence Victims." *Domestic Violence Report* 5, no. 2 (December/January 2000): 17–18, 26–29. Reprinted in Lemon, Nancy K. D. *Domestic Violence Law*, 821–22. Eagan, MN: West Group, 2001.

Shaw, Lois, and Catherine Hill. *The Gender Gap in Pension Coverage: What Does the Future Hold?* IWPR Publication E507. Washington, DC: Institute for Women's Policy Research, 2002.

Simpson, A. W. B. *A History of the Land Law*. 2nd ed. Oxford: Oxford University Press, 1896.

U.S. General Accounting Office. *Domestic Violence: Prevalence and Implications for Employment among Welfare Recipients*. Washington, DC: Author, 1998.

Walsh, Sharon. "For Corporate Spouses, an Unlimited Partnership." *Washington Post*, January 4, 1998.

INDEX